THE NIV

Serendipity

BIBLE STUDY BOOK
OF
ACTS

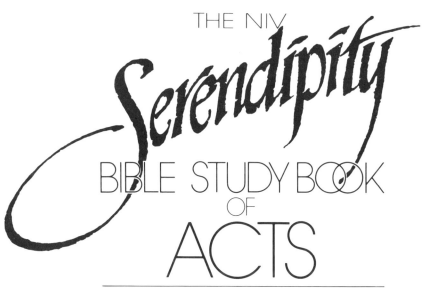

THE NIV Serendipity

BIBLE STUDY BOOK OF ACTS

STUDY QUESTIONS WITH NEW INTERNATIONAL VERSION TEXT

EDITED BY
LYMAN COLEMAN, DENNY RYDBERG,
RICHARD PEACE, GARY CHRISTOPHERSON

Lamplighter
Books Grand Rapids,
Michigan
Zondervan Publishing House

The NIV Serendipity Bible Study Book of Acts
Excerpted from *The Serendipity Bible Study Book*
Originally published
by Zondervan Publishing House
Copyright © 1986 by Serendipity House

and

The Holy Bible,
New International Version (North American Edition)
Copyright © 1973, 1978, 1984 by International Bible Society.
Used by permission of Zondervan Bible Publishers

Lamplighter Books are published by the Zondervan Publishing House
1415 Lake Drive, S.E., Grand Rapids, Michigan 49506

Library of Congress Cataloging in Publication Data

Bible. N.T. Acts. English. New International. 1988.
The NIV serendipity Bible study book of Acts.

"Lamplighter books."
1. Bible. N.T. Acts—Textbooks. I. Coleman, Lyman. II. Title.
BS2623.C66   1989   226'.6'0076   88–5602
ISBN 0-310-59011-6

Edited by Janet Kobobel and Lavonne Neff

Printed in the United States of America

89   90   91   92   93 / CH / 10   9   8   7   6   5   4   3   2   1

HOW TO USE THIS BOOKLET

COMBINES THE BIBLICAL BOOK OF ACTS WITH

1. Contemporary introduction and summary of Acts
2. The full NIV text of Acts
3. Discussion questions in the margin

DESIGNED FOR GROUPS OF ALL AGES

If you can make coffee (or find someone who can), you can lead a Bible study with this booklet. The questions guide the sharing from fun, get-acquainted discussion to more thought-provoking responses at the close.

This booklet is designed for all kinds of groups:

- Your family
- Singles' groups
- Youth groups
- Men's groups

- Bible study groups
- Couples' groups
- Women's groups
- Church-wide study groups

You don't need a college degree in group techniques or a seminary degree in Bible to be a leader. The tools are right here to lead a Bible study group. Compare what you read next with the illustrated page that follows.

HERE'S HOW TO LEAD A GROUP

1. Divide into clusters of four or five people.
2. Ask one person in each small group of four to be the leader.
3. Make sure everyone has a booklet. Ask everyone to turn to the beginning.
4. Have each group start with one or two of the OPEN questions, which are designed to break the ice and get the group talking. (Don't let the child-like nature of the questions fool you. There is a purpose in starting this way.)
5. After 10 minutes, call time and read the Scripture passage together.
6. Move to the DIG questions. Have the leader of each group ask one person to answer question 1, the next person answer question 2, the next person question 3, and so on.
7. After 15 or 20 minutes, call time and move on.
8. Ask the group to move to the REFLECT questions. The study converges here into an in-depth sharing experience. Suggest that each group concentrate on one or two REFLECT questions that are relevant to those in the group.
9. Close in prayer.

FEATURING READY-MADE BIBLE STUDIES

QUESTIONS IN THE MARGIN

1. TO OPEN
Questions to
break the ice and
start the sharing.

2. TO DIG
Questions to
study the Bible
passage and share.

3. TO REFLECT
Questions to
apply the passage
to your life.

QUESTIONS	NIV TEXT

1. OPEN: **1.** If you had a year's wages to blow on one extravagant gift, what would you buy? **2.** What is one special gift you remember receiving for your birthday or at Christmas time when you were a child?

2. DIG: **1.** What was significant about this time of year? How might this cause the fear expressed by Jesus' opponents? **2.** Does this passage teach that it is wrong to give to the poor? Why would it have been wrong in this instance? **3.** What effect do you think the events in this passage had on Judas' decision in verses 10-11?

3. REFLECT: **1.** For what would you like to be remembered? **2.** If you had a year's wages to give to the cause of Christ, to whom would you give it? What's keeping you from giving part of it now? **3.** If Jesus came to your house tonight, what gift would you want to give him? **4.** In what ways are you similar to and different from the officials, Judas, Simon, and the woman?

OPEN: **1.** What is one of your favorite places to eat? What makes this place special? **2.** What are some happy childhood memories of mealtimes?

DIG: **1.** How do you think the disciples felt about Jesus' words in verse 18? What would this do to the mood of the Passover meal? What tone is Jesus trying to set for this meal? Why? **2.** What do you know about the origins of the Passover meal (see Exod. 12)? **3.** What new meaning did Jesus give to the Passover bread? the wine? What vow did he make? **4.** How much do you think the disciples understood when Jesus spoke about his body and blood? **5.** How do you think the disciples felt as they sang a hymn and

Jesus Anointed at Bethany

14 Now the Passover and the Feast of Unleavened Bread were only two days away, and the chief priests and the teachers of the law were looking for some sly way to arrest Jesus and kill him. [2]"But not during the Feast," they said, "or the people may riot."

[3]While he was in Bethany, reclining at the table in the home of a man known as Simon the Leper, a woman came with an alabaster jar of very expensive perfume, made of pure nard. She broke the jar and poured the perfume on his head.

[4]Some of those present were saying indignantly to one another, "Why this waste of perfume? [5]It could have been sold for more than a year's wages and the money given to the poor." And they rebuked her harshly.

[6]"Leave her alone," said Jesus. "Why are you bothering her? She has done a beautiful thing to me. [7]The poor you will always have with you, and you can help them any time you want. But you will not always have me. [8]She did what she could. She poured perfume on my body beforehand to prepare for my burial. [9]I tell you the truth, wherever the gospel is preached throughout the world, what she has done will also be told, in memory of her."

[10]Then Judas Iscariot, one of the Twelve, went to the chief priests to betray Jesus to them. [11]They were delighted to hear this and promised to give him money. So he watched for an opportunity to hand him over.

The Lord's Supper

[12]On the first day of the Feast of Unleavened Bread, when it was customary to sacrifice the Passover lamb, Jesus' disciples asked him, "Where do you want us to go and make preparations for you to eat the Passover?"

[13]So he sent two of his disciples, telling them, "Go into the city, and a man carrying a jar of water will meet you. Follow him. [14]Say to the owner of the house he enters, 'The Teacher asks: Where is my guest room, where I may eat the Passover with my disciples?' [15]He will show you a large upper room, furnished and ready. Make preparations for us there."

[16]The disciples left, went into the city and found things just as Jesus had told them. So they prepared the Passover.

[17]When evening came, Jesus arrived with the Twelve. [18]While they were reclining at the table eating, he said, "I tell you the truth, one of you will betray me—one who is eating with me."

[19]They were saddened, and one by one they said to him,

"For where two or three
come together
in my name,
there am I with them."

Matthew 18:20 NIV

PREFACE

THE NEW INTERNATIONAL VERSION is a completely new translation of the Holy Bible made by over a hundred scholars working directly from the best available Hebrew, Aramaic and Greek texts. It had its beginning in 1965 when, after several years of exploratory study by committees from the Christian Reformed Church and the National Association of Evangelicals, a group of scholars met at Palos Heights, Illinois, and concurred in the need for a new translation of the Bible in contemporary English. This group, though not made up of official church representatives, was transdenominational. Its conclusion was endorsed by a large number of leaders from many denominations who met in Chicago in 1966.

Responsibility for the new version was delegated by the Palos Heights group to a self-governing body of fifteen, the Committee on Bible Translation, composed for the most part of biblical scholars from colleges, universities and seminaries. In 1967 the New York Bible Society (now the International Bible Society) generously undertook the financial sponsorship of the project—a sponsorship that made it possible to enlist the help of many distinguished scholars. The fact that participants from the United States, Great Britain, Canada, Australia and New Zealand worked together gave the project its international scope. That they were from many denominations—including Anglican, Assemblies of God, Baptist, Brethren, Christian Reformed, Church of Christ, Evangelical Free, Lutheran, Mennonite, Methodist, Nazarene, Presbyterian, Wesleyan and other churches—helped to safeguard the translation from sectarian bias.

How it was made helps to give the New International Version its distinctiveness. The translation of each book was assigned to a team of scholars. Next, one of the Intermediate Editorial Committees revised the initial translation, with constant reference to the Hebrew, Aramaic or Greek. Their work then went to one of the General Editorial Committees, which checked it in detail and made another thorough revision. This revision in turn was carefully reviewed by the Committee on Bible Translation, which made further changes and then released the final version for publication. In this way the entire Bible underwent three revisions, during each of which the translation was examined for its faithfulness to the original languages and for its English style.

All this involved many thousands of hours of research and discussion regarding the meaning of the texts and the precise way of putting them into English. It may well be that no other translation has been made by a more thorough process of review and revision from committee to committee than this one.

From the beginning of the project, the Committee on Bible Translation held to certain goals for the New International Version: that it would be an accurate translation and one that would have clarity and literary quality and so prove suitable for public and private reading, teaching, preaching, memorizing and liturgical use. The Committee also sought to preserve some measure of continuity with the long tradition of translating the Scriptures into English.

In working toward these goals, the translators were united in their commitment to the authority and infallibility of the Bible as God's Word in written form. They believe that it contains the divine answer to the deepest needs of humanity, that it sheds unique light on our path in a dark world, and that it sets forth the way to our eternal well-being.

The first concern of the translators has been the accuracy of the translation and its fidelity to the thought of the biblical writers. They have weighed the significance of the lexical and grammatical details of the Hebrew, Aramaic and Greek texts. At the same time, they have striven for more than a word-for-word translation. Because thought patterns and syntax differ from language to language, faithful communication of the meaning of the writers of the Bible demands frequent modifications in sentence structure and constant regard for the contextual meanings of words.

A sensitive feeling for style does not always accompany scholarship. Accordingly the Committee on Bible Translation submitted the developing version to a number of stylistic consultants. Two of them read every book of both Old and New Testaments twice—once before and once after the last major revision—and made invaluable suggestions. Samples of the translation were tested for clarity and ease of reading by various kinds of people—young and old, highly educated and less well educated, ministers and laymen.

Concern for clear and natural English—that the New International Version should be idiomatic but not idiosyncratic, contemporary but not dated—motivated the translators and consultants. At the same time, they tried to reflect the differing styles of the biblical writers. In view of the international use of English, the translators sought to avoid obvious Americanisms on the one hand and obvious Anglicisms on the other. A British edition reflects the comparatively few differences of significant idiom and of spelling.

As for the traditional pronouns "thou," "thee" and "thine" in reference to the Deity, the translators judged that to use these archaisms (along with the old verb forms such as "doest," "wouldest" and "hadst") would violate accuracy in translation. Neither Hebrew, Aramaic nor Greek uses special pronouns for the persons of the Godhead. A present-day translation is not enhanced by forms that in the time of the King James Version were used in everyday speech, whether referring to God or man.

For the Old Testament the standard Hebrew text, the Masoretic Text as published in the latest editions of *Biblia Hebraica,* was used throughout. The Dead Sea Scrolls contain material bearing on an earlier stage of the Hebrew text. They were consulted, as were the Samaritan Pentateuch and the ancient scribal traditions relating to textual changes. Sometimes a variant Hebrew reading in the margin of the Masoretic Text was followed instead of the text itself. Such instances, being variants within the Masoretic tradition, are not specified by footnotes. In rare cases, words in the consonantal text were divided differently from the way they appear in the Masoretic Text. Footnotes indicate this. The translators also consulted the more important early versions—the Septuagint; Aquila, Symmachus and Theodotion; the Vulgate; the Syriac Peshitta; the Targums; and for the Psalms the *Juxta Hebraica* of Jerome. Readings from these versions were occasionally followed where the Masoretic Text seemed doubtful and where accepted principles of textual criticism showed that one or more of these textual witnesses appeared to provide the correct reading. Such instances are footnoted. Sometimes vowel letters and vowel signs did not, in the judgment of the translators, represent the correct vowels for the original consonantal text. Accordingly some words were read with a different set of vowels. These instances are usually not indicated by footnotes.

The Greek text used in translating the New Testament was an eclectic one. No other piece of ancient literature has such an abundance of manuscript witnesses as does the New Testament. Where existing manuscripts differ, the translators made their choice of readings according to accepted principles of New Testament textual criticism. Footnotes call attention to places where there was uncertainty about what the original text was. The best current printed texts of the Greek New Testament were used.

There is a sense in which the work of translation is never wholly finished. This applies to all great literature and uniquely so to the Bible. In 1973 the New Testament in the New International Version was published. Since then, suggestions for corrections and revisions have been received from various sources. The Committee on Bible Translation carefully considered the suggestions and adopted a number of them. These were incorporated in the first printing of the entire Bible in 1978. Additional revisions were made by the Committee on Bible Translation in 1983 and appear in printings after that date.

As in other ancient documents, the precise meaning of the biblical texts is sometimes uncertain. This is more often the case with the Hebrew and Aramaic texts than with the Greek text. Although archaeological and linguistic discoveries in this century aid in understanding difficult passages, some uncertainties remain. The more significant of these have been called to the reader's attention in the footnotes.

In regard to the divine name *YHWH*, commonly referred to as the *Tetragrammaton*, the translators adopted the device used in most English versions of rendering that name as "LORD" in capital letters to distinguish it from *Adonai*, another Hebrew word rendered "Lord," for which small letters are used. Wherever the two names stand together in the Old Testament as a compound name of God, they are rendered "Sovereign LORD."

Because for most readers today the phrases "the LORD of hosts" and "God of hosts" have little meaning, this version renders them "the LORD Almighty" and "God Almighty." These renderings convey the sense of the Hebrew, namely, "he who is sovereign over all the 'hosts' (powers) in heaven and on earth, especially over the 'hosts' (armies) of Israel." For readers unacquainted with Hebrew this does not make clear the distinction between *Sabaoth* ("hosts" or "Almighty") and *Shaddai* (which can also be translated "Almighty"), but the latter occurs infrequently and is always footnoted. When *Adonai* and *YHWH Sabaoth* occur together, they are rendered "the Lord, the LORD Almighty."

As for other proper nouns, the familiar spellings of the King James Version are generally retained. Names traditionally spelled with "ch," except where it is final, are usually spelled in this translation with "k" or "c," since the biblical languages do not have the sound that "ch" frequently indicates in English—for example, in *chant*. For well-known names such as Zechariah, however, the traditional spelling has been retained. Variation in the spelling of names in the original languages has usually not been indicated. Where a person or place has two or more different names in the Hebrew, Aramaic or Greek texts, the more familiar one has generally been used, with footnotes where needed.

To achieve clarity the translators sometimes supplied words not in the original texts but required by the context. If there was uncertainty about such material, it is enclosed in brackets. Also for the sake of clarity or style, nouns, including some proper nouns, are sometimes substituted for pronouns, and vice versa. And though the Hebrew writers often shifted back and forth between first, second and third personal pronouns without change of antecedent, this translation often makes them uniform, in accordance with English style and without the use of footnotes.

Poetical passages are printed as poetry, that is, with indentation of lines and with separate stanzas. These are generally designed to reflect the structure of Hebrew poetry. This poetry is normally characterized by parallelism in balanced lines. Most of the poetry in the Bible is in the Old Testament, and scholars differ regarding the scansion of Hebrew lines. The translators determined the stanza divisions for the most part by analysis of the subject matter. The stanzas therefore serve as poetic paragraphs.

As an aid to the reader, italicized sectional headings are inserted in most of the books. They are not to be regarded as part of the NIV text, are not for oral reading, and are not intended to dictate the interpretation of the sections they head.

The footnotes in this version are of several kinds, most of which need no explanation. Those giving alternative translations begin with "Or" and generally introduce the alternative with the last word preceding it in the text, except when it is a single-word alternative; in poetry quoted in a footnote a slant mark indicates a line division. Footnotes introduced by "Or" do not have uniform significance. In some cases two possible translations were considered to have about equal validity. In other cases, though the translators were convinced that the translation in the text was correct, they judged that another interpretation was possible and of sufficient importance to be represented in a footnote.

In the New Testament, footnotes that refer to uncertainty regarding the original text are introduced by "Some manuscripts" or similar expressions. In the Old Testament, evidence for the reading chosen is given first and evidence for the alternative is added after a semicolon (for example: Septuagint; Hebrew *father*). In such notes the term "Hebrew" refers to the Masoretic Text.

It should be noted that minerals, flora and fauna, architectural details, articles of clothing and jewelry, musical instruments and other articles cannot always be identified with precision. Also measures of capacity in the biblical period are particularly uncertain (see the table of weights and measures following the text).

Like all translations of the Bible, made as they are by imperfect man, this one undoubtedly falls short of its goals. Yet we are grateful to God for the extent to which he has enabled us to realize these goals and for the strength he has given us and our colleagues to complete our task. We offer this version of the Bible to him in whose name and for whose glory it has been made. We pray that it will lead many into a better understanding of the Holy Scriptures and a fuller knowledge of Jesus Christ the incarnate Word, of whom the Scriptures so faithfully testify.

The Committee on Bible Translation

June 1978
(Revised August 1983)

Names of the translators and editors may be secured from the International Bible Society P.O. Box 62970, Colorado Springs, Colorado 80962-2970.

ACTS

INTRODUCTION

Author

Although Luke is nowhere named within Acts as author, there is a strong and ancient tradition that he did, indeed, write this book as a companion piece to the third Gospel.

Little is known of Luke. He is mentioned only three times in the New Testament (Col. 4:14; Philem. 24; 2 Tim. 4:11). From these references, it can be deduced that Luke was a physician, a valued companion of Paul, and a Gentile.

A Physician

Luke's medical background is corroborated by his use of medical terms (especially in his gospel), for example, in recounting the story of the camel and the needle's eye. "For the word needle both Mark and Matthew use the Greek word *raphis,* which is the ordinary word for a tailor's or a household needle. Luke alone uses the word *belone,* which is the technical word for a surgeons' needle" (William Barclay, *The Acts of the Apostles,* p. XIV).

Paul's Companion

Luke's role as Paul's traveling companion is evident in the Book of Acts. In the four so-called *we* sections, the author suddenly switches from saying "They did this" to "We did that" (Acts 16:10-17; 20: 5-6; 21:1-18; 27:1-28:16). At these points in Paul's journeys, Luke joined him as a colleague in ministry.

A Gentile

We learn that Luke was a Gentile from the list of greetings with which Paul concludes Colossians. First Paul records the greetings sent by "the only Jews among my fellow workers" (Col. 4:10-11). Then in verse 12 he begins a second set of greetings presumably from the Gentiles in the party. Luke's name is included in this latter list.

Characteristics

The Book of Acts is the bridge between the Gospels and the Epistles. It is no accident that modern Bibles are arranged with the life of Jesus on one side of Acts and the correspondence of the apostles on the other. This is because, on the one hand, Acts completes the story of Jesus. It shows how his life, death, and resurrection brought a whole new community into existence: the church. On the other hand, Acts sets the stage for the correspondence to this church; the letters make up the rest of the New Testament. At many points it would be difficult to get the full sense of what the Epistles are saying without the data found in Acts.

Luke tells the story of the development of the church, not by strictly chronicling every event that occurred as the church spread from Jerusalem to Rome — the sheer volume of the data prevented this — but rather by opening a series of windows that allows us to glimpse important (and representative) developments in its growth.

1. Key Figure—The Holy Spirit

One thing that characterizes the entire story is the work of the Holy Spirit. There is little question in Luke's mind how the church spread: The Holy Spirit did it. So we see the church come into being as a result of the baptism of the Holy Spirit (2:38-41). First as only a handful of disciples, it turned suddenly into a full-fledged movement. We then see the Holy Spirit gently but directly guide the early church (13:2 and 16:7). In fact, the presence of the Holy Spirit signals that a church is authentic and not spurious (19:1-6). Some have suggested that this book ought to have been labeled *The Acts of the Holy Spirit* and not *The Acts of the Apostles*!

2. Leading Roles—Peter and Paul

This latter designation is inaccurate for yet another reason. The whole apostolic band is not really in view here. The Book of Acts is the story of only two apostles—Peter and Paul. Peter's story is told first. In the initial 12 chapters, he is the central figure. But in chapter 13, the spotlight shifts to Paul, and he holds center stage until Acts concludes.

The stories of these two men are not dissimilar. In fact, there are a surprising number of common elements. Both heal cripples (3:1-10; 14:8-12); both have the experience of seeing cures brought about in unusual ways (5:15-16; 19:11-12); both bring people back to life (9:36-42; 20:9-12); both meet a magician (8:9-25; 13:6-12); and both are released from prison as the result of a miracle (12:7; 16:26-28).

The reason for this focus on Peter and on Paul is not hard to guess. They were the key leaders of the two main elements of the early church: Peter was the chief apostle to the Jews, while Paul was the chief apostle to the Gentiles. So in hearing their stories, we hear the story of the unfolding of the whole church.

3. Key Sources

Where did Luke get his information about the growth of the church? The source of the second half of the book (chapters 13-28) is clear. Luke got this information directly from his friend and companion Paul. We know Luke was actually with Paul during some of this period (the *we* sections), and he may well have kept a journal. We can also guess that during the long days of travel, and during Paul's confinement in prison, the great apostle probably recounted his many adventures to Luke. But what about the first twelve chapters that center around Peter? Here is where Luke's skill as a historian is especially evident. Luke tells us in his prologue to the third Gospel that he "carefully investigated everything from the beginning" (Luke 1:3). How? Probably by talking to many individuals he may have met via Paul. For example, Luke knew Mark. Both men were with Paul when he wrote Colossians (Col. 4:10, 14). From Mark he would have received valuable information about the growth of the church in Jerusalem and about Peter's role in this. (Many feel Mark's gospel reflects Peter's perspective.) And certainly Luke would have listened to the stories about Peter that were repeated in the churches he visited. Finally, he may well have had access to the official records (written and oral) of the key churches mentioned in the first twelve chapters—the church at Jerusalem (from Mark and others); the church at Caesarea (Philip and his daughters entertained Luke and Paul according to Acts 21:8, and Philip was associated with Stephen and the events of Acts 6:1-8:3); and the church at Antioch (many feel Luke's home was Antioch).

4. Keen Historian

Luke's accuracy as a historian was called into question by certain scholars until the archaeological research of Sir William Ramsay demonstrated Luke's exact and detailed knowledge of the political and social conditions of the times. For example, although a number of different titles were given to Roman officials, Luke always seems to have got it right. When Paul was in Cyprus (Acts 13:7), Luke tells us a proconsul was in charge, although this was only briefly the case. At Malta (Acts 28:7), the ruler is correctly called the "chief man" or "chief official" *protos*. At Ephesus (Acts 19:35), Luke identifies the official who quieted the crowd as the "city clerk" *grammateus*. In Thessolonica (Acts 17:6), he identifies the leaders as "city officials" *politarches*, even though this was an unusual office with no parallel elsewhere in the Roman Empire and only recently verified by inscriptions. Luke had the mind of a researcher: He was careful and paid attention to details. Thus when reading his story of the early church, we have confidence that what Luke tells us is just what happened.

Theme

Why did Luke write the Book of Acts? One reason must have been his desire to commend Christianity to the Gentile world in general and to the Roman government in particular. Certainly there was much about Christianity that would have appealed to Gentiles. For one thing, Jesus came for all people and not just for his Jewish kinfolk. So one finds in Acts the same universality present in Luke's gospel. The good news about Jesus is not just for Jews but for all people. Not surprisingly, therefore, we find in Acts not only Jews turning to Jesus (three thousand on the Day of Pentecost, Acts 2:41) but also Gentiles. We see Peter (the Apostle to the Jews) welcoming Cornelius, the Roman centurion, into the church. We see Philip preaching to the Samaritans and Jewish believers and evangelizing Gentiles in Antioch. In particular, we find Paul called by Christ to be the Apostle to the Gentiles, setting up churches across the Roman Empire. Finally in Acts 15, there is formal affirmation that Gentiles are accepted in the church of Jesus Christ on equal terms with Jews (they do not first have to become Jewish converts). Acts is an eloquent testimony to the universal appeal of Jesus.

Luke's response to the Roman government is fascinating. He seemed to go out of his way to show that Christians were loyal citizens and not lawbreakers and criminals (18:14; 19:37; 23:29; 25:25). He also took pains to point out that Roman officials had always treated Christians fairly and courteously (13:12; 16:35-40; 18:12-17; 19:31). This was important to state lest Christianity be perceived as a political movement and therefore a threat to the Roman Empire. His writing did, after all, talk about the kingdom and about Jesus as Lord (the imperial title).

However, commending Christianity to Gentiles was probably not Luke's central aim. His main purpose is implicit in 1:8. "But you will receive power when the Holy Spirit comes on you; and you will be my witnesses in Jerusalem, and in all Judea and Samaria, and to the ends of the earth." Luke's aim was to show how, in thirty short years, Christianity had spread from Jerusalem to Rome.

Structure

Luke accomplished his purpose by describing six phases of growth (as charted by C. H. Turner and noted in Barclay, *The Acts of the Apostles,* p. xviii):

1. *The church at Jerusalem* (1:1-6:7). Summary statement: "So the word of God spread. The number of disciples in Jerusalem increased rapidly, and a large number of priests became obedient to the faith" (6:7).
2. *From Jerusalem to Palestine* (6:8-9:31). Summary statement: "Then the church throughout Judea, Galilee and Samaria enjoyed a time of peace . . . it grew in numbers . . ." (9:31).
3. *From Palestine to Antioch, gateway to the Gentile world* (9:32-12:24). Summary statement: "The word of God continued to increase and spread" (12:24).
4. *From Antioch to Asia* (12:25-16:5). Summary statement: "So the churches were strengthened in the faith and grew daily in numbers" (16:5).
5. *From Asia to Europe* (16:6-19:20). Summary statement: "In this way the word of the Lord spread widely and grew in power" (19:20).
6. *From Europe in general to Rome in particular* (19:21-28:31). Summary statement: "Therefore I want you to know that God's salvation has been sent to the Gentiles, and they will listen!" (28:28).

Acts

DIG: 1. Read the last chapter of Luke. How does the last chapter of Luke relate to Acts 1:1-11? What does this tell you about the relationship between these two books? 2. What is the importance of the Resurrection to the Christian church? Why is it important that there be proofs of the Resurrection? 3. What kind of kingdom are the disciples looking for in verse 6? What does this tell you about their understanding of Jesus' kingdom? Is this surprising to you? Why or why not? 4. What are the two main parts of verse 8? How are they interrelated? Which comes first? Why? In what way does verse 8 introduce the Book of Acts? 5. What does verse 8 tell you about the nature of God's kingdom? How does this contrast with the disciples' view in verse 6?

REFLECT: 1. What proofs do you have of Jesus' resurrection? How confident do you feel when you communicate these truths to non-believers? 2. What is your "Jerusalem . . . to the ends of the earth"? How do you help to establish the kingdom in your world? What role does the Holy Spirit play in this?

OPEN: What memories do you have of not being elected to a position or chosen to a team? How do you feel about it now?

DIG: 1. Who are the key people mentioned in verses 13-14? What do you know about each of these individuals? How have Jesus' brothers changed over the course of Jesus' ministry? What do you think caused this change? Why? 2. What seems to be Peter's role in this group? Does this surprise you? Why or why not? 3. Why would it be necessary for there to be twelve main disciples? What do the passages Peter quotes from Psalms have to do with this? 4. What were the qualifications to be met by the two candidates? How would these qualifications help to fulfill the goal of the disciples' ministry? 5. What part does prayer have in this passage? How important does prayer seem to be to Jesus' followers? Why would prayer be more important for them now than before?

Jesus Taken Up Into Heaven

1 In my former book, Theophilus, I wrote about all that Jesus began to do and to teach ²until the day he was taken up to heaven, after giving instructions through the Holy Spirit to the apostles he had chosen. ³After his suffering, he showed himself to these men and gave many convincing proofs that he was alive. He appeared to them over a period of forty days and spoke about the kingdom of God. ⁴On one occasion, while he was eating with them, he gave them this command: "Do not leave Jerusalem, but wait for the gift my Father promised, which you have heard me speak about. ⁵For John baptized with*a* water, but in a few days you will be baptized with the Holy Spirit."

⁶So when they met together, they asked him, "Lord, are you at this time going to restore the kingdom to Israel?"

⁷He said to them: "It is not for you to know the times or dates the Father has set by his own authority. ⁸But you will receive power when the Holy Spirit comes on you; and you will be my witnesses in Jerusalem, and in all Judea and Samaria, and to the ends of the earth."

⁹After he said this, he was taken up before their very eyes, and a cloud hid him from their sight.

¹⁰They were looking intently up into the sky as he was going, when suddenly two men dressed in white stood beside them. ¹¹"Men of Galilee," they said, "why do you stand here looking into the sky? This same Jesus, who has been taken from you into heaven, will come back in the same way you have seen him go into heaven."

Matthias Chosen to Replace Judas

¹²Then they returned to Jerusalem from the hill called the Mount of Olives, a Sabbath day's walk*b* from the city. ¹³When they arrived, they went upstairs to the room where they were staying. Those present were Peter, John, James and Andrew; Philip and Thomas, Bartholomew and Matthew; James son of Alphaeus and Simon the Zealot, and Judas son of James. ¹⁴They all joined together constantly in prayer, along with the women and Mary the mother of Jesus, and with his brothers.

¹⁵In those days Peter stood up among the believers*c* (a group numbering about a hundred and twenty) ¹⁶and said, "Brothers, the Scripture had to be fulfilled which the Holy Spirit spoke long ago through the mouth of David concerning Judas, who served as guide for those who arrested Jesus— ¹⁷he was one of our number and shared in this ministry."

¹⁸(With the reward he got for his wickedness, Judas bought a field; there he fell headlong, his body burst open and all his intestines spilled out. ¹⁹Everyone in Jerusalem heard about this, so they called that field in their language Akeldama, that is, Field of Blood.)

---

a5 Or *in*   *b12* That is, about 3/4 mile (about 1,100 meters)   *c15* Greek *brothers*

[20]"For," said Peter, "it is written in the book of Psalms,

" 'May his place be deserted;
let there be no one to dwell in it,'[d]

and,

" 'May another take his place of leadership.'[e]

[21]Therefore it is necessary to choose one of the men who have been with us the whole time the Lord Jesus went in and out among us, [22]beginning from John's baptism to the time when Jesus was taken up from us. For one of these must become a witness with us of his resurrection."

[23]So they proposed two men: Joseph called Barsabbas (also known as Justus) and Matthias. [24]Then they prayed, "Lord, you know everyone's heart. Show us which of these two you have chosen [25]to take over this apostolic ministry, which Judas left to go where he belongs." [26]Then they cast lots, and the lot fell to Matthias; so he was added to the eleven apostles.

The Holy Spirit Comes at Pentecost

2 When the day of Pentecost came, they were all together in one place. [2]Suddenly a sound like the blowing of a violent wind came from heaven and filled the whole house where they were sitting. [3]They saw what seemed to be tongues of fire that separated and came to rest on each of them. [4]All of them were filled with the Holy Spirit and began to speak in other tongues[f] as the Spirit enabled them.

[5]Now there were staying in Jerusalem God-fearing Jews from every nation under heaven. [6]When they heard this sound, a crowd came together in bewilderment, because each one heard them speaking in his own language. [7]Utterly amazed, they asked: "Are not all these men who are speaking Galileans? [8]Then how is it that each of us hears them in his own native language? [9]Parthians, Medes and Elamites; residents of Mesopotamia, Judea and Cappadocia, Pontus and Asia, [10]Phrygia and Pamphylia, Egypt and the parts of Libya near Cyrene; visitors from Rome [11](both Jews and converts to Judaism); Cretans and Arabs—we hear them declaring the wonders of God in our own tongues!" [12]Amazed and perplexed, they asked one another, "What does this mean?"

[13]Some, however, made fun of them and said, "They have had too much wine.[g]"

Peter Addresses the Crowd

[14]Then Peter stood up with the Eleven, raised his voice and addressed the crowd: "Fellow Jews and all of you who live in Jerusalem, let me explain this to you; listen carefully to what I say. [15]These men are not drunk, as you suppose. It's only nine in the morning! [16]No, this is what was spoken by the prophet Joel:

REFLECT: 1. Who are your spiritual soul mates—brothers and sisters with whom you share a great deal spiritually? How have they encouraged you in the past six months? 2. How would you describe your prayer life? Where do you do most of your praying? How often do you pray with others? What has God taught you about prayer in the last year? 3. How does your church choose leaders? How does that compare with the way Matthias was selected? Why the difference? In what ways would you like to improve the leadership selection in your church?

OPEN: If you could learn one foreign language today, which would you choose? Why?

DIG: 1. What do you know about Pentecost (also called the Feast of Harvest, Exod. 23:16, or the Feast of Weeks, Deut. 16:9-10)? Why is it appropriate that the Holy Spirit was given on Pentecost? 2. What seems to be the purpose for the Holy Spirit's gift of tongues? Is this purpose achieved? How does the message of the disciples help to achieve it?

REFLECT: 1. Where is your upper room—the place where God seemed to empower you in a special way? What happened? How has it changed your life? 2. What do you think was God's part and Jesus' followers' part in this event? How can you prepare yourself for God's work? What do you need to do this week to be better prepared for God's use?

OPEN: What's the largest crowd you've ever spoken to? How did you feel just before you spoke? How well did you do?

DIG: 1. How does Peter seize the opportunity of the moment? Why do you think he seizes this opportunity? What does this tell you about Peter? 2. Read Luke 22:54-62. What has brought about the change in Peter between that night in the courtyard and this morning of Pentecost? 3. How much of the sermon is prophetic

---

d20 Psalm 69:25   *e20* Psalm 109:8   *f4* Or *languages*; also in verse 11
g13 Or *sweet wine*

Scriptures? Why would this be important to Peter's audience? **4.** How does the portion of Joel in verses 17-21 explain the phenomenon of tongues? How does it serve to introduce the next passage? **5.** What importance does Peter give to the Resurrection in his sermon? Why would it be important for Peter to establish the truth of the Resurrection? How would David's prophecies help him to do this? **6.** How would David's position as king help Peter to establish Jesus as Lord? **7.** Make an outline of Peter's sermon in verses 14-36. Based on your outline, what is the purpose of Peter's sermon? How do each of the main parts of this sermon build toward this purpose? Based on this purpose, what would be a good title for this sermon? **8.** Is this a successful sermon? Why or why not? What do you think are the ingredients of its success? Why these ingredients? How does this sermon help to carry out Jesus' words in Acts 1:8?

REFLECT: 1. When was the last time you seized an opportunity to witness for Jesus? What happened? Who stood with you at that time? **2.** What impresses you most about Peter in this section—his courage, his knowledge, etc.? How are you like Peter? Unlike him? What is God suggesting to you as you watch Peter in these verses? What encourages you as you watch Peter? Why? **3.** What facts about Jesus do you think are most important in helping nonbelievers come to faith? **4.** How important is fulfilled prophecy to your confidence in the Christian faith? Why? **5.** When did you make your initial commitment to Jesus Christ? Who was influential in this decision? What did that person say that helped convince you of your need for Jesus Christ? **6.** What are some of your spiritual dreams or visions? How is God helping you to realize these dreams?

[17]" 'In the last days, God says,
I will pour out my Spirit on all people.
Your sons and daughters will prophesy,
your young men will see visions,
your old men will dream dreams.
[18]Even on my servants, both men and women,
I will pour out my Spirit in those days,
and they will prophesy.
[19]I will show wonders in the heaven above
and signs on the earth below,
blood and fire and billows of smoke.
[20]The sun will be turned to darkness
and the moon to blood
before the coming of the great and glorious day of the Lord.
[21]And everyone who calls
on the name of the Lord will be saved.'[h]

[22]"Men of Israel, listen to this: Jesus of Nazareth was a man accredited by God to you by miracles, wonders and signs, which God did among you through him, as you yourselves know. [23]This man was handed over to you by God's set purpose and foreknowledge; and you, with the help of wicked men,[i] put him to death by nailing him to the cross. [24]But God raised him from the dead, freeing him from the agony of death, because it was impossible for death to keep its hold on him. [25]David said about him:

" 'I saw the Lord always before me.
Because he is at my right hand,
I will not be shaken.
[26]Therefore my heart is glad and my tongue rejoices;
my body also will live in hope,
[27]because you will not abandon me to the grave,
nor will you let your Holy One see decay.
[28]You have made known to me the paths of life;
you will fill me with joy in your presence.'[j]

[29]"Brothers, I can tell you confidently that the patriarch David died and was buried, and his tomb is here to this day. [30]But he was a prophet and knew that God had promised him on oath that he would place one of his descendants on his throne. [31]Seeing what was ahead, he spoke of the resurrection of the Christ,[k] that he was not abandoned to the grave, nor did his body see decay. [32]God has raised this Jesus to life, and we are all witnesses of the fact. [33]Exalted to the right hand of God, he has received from the Father the promised Holy Spirit and has poured out what you now see and hear. [34]For David did not ascend to heaven, and yet he said,

" 'The Lord said to my Lord:
"Sit at my right hand

h21 Joel 2:28-32   *i23* Or *of those not having the law* (that is, Gentiles)
j28 Psalm 16:8-11   *k31* Or *Messiah.* "The Christ" (Greek) and "the Messiah" (Hebrew) both mean "the Anointed One"; also in verse 36.

[35]until I make your enemies
a footstool for your feet." "[l]

[36]"Therefore let all Israel be assured of this: God has made this Jesus, whom you crucified, both Lord and Christ."

[37]When the people heard this, they were cut to the heart and said to Peter and the other apostles, "Brothers, what shall we do?"

[38]Peter replied, "Repent and be baptized, every one of you, in the name of Jesus Christ for the forgiveness of your sins. And you will receive the gift of the Holy Spirit. [39]The promise is for you and your children and for all who are far off—for all whom the Lord our God will call."

[40]With many other words he warned them; and he pleaded with them, "Save yourselves from this corrupt generation." [41]Those who accepted his message were baptized, and about three thousand were added to their number that day.

The Fellowship of the Believers

[42]They devoted themselves to the apostles' teaching and to the fellowship, to the breaking of bread and to prayer. [43]Everyone was filled with awe, and many wonders and miraculous signs were done by the apostles. [44]All the believers were together and had everything in common. [45]Selling their possessions and goods, they gave to anyone as he had need. [46]Every day they continued to meet together in the temple courts. They broke bread in their homes and ate together with glad and sincere hearts, [47]praising God and enjoying the favor of all the people. And the Lord added to their number daily those who were being saved.

Peter Heals the Crippled Beggar

3 One day Peter and John were going up to the temple at the time of prayer—at three in the afternoon. [2]Now a man crippled from birth was being carried to the temple gate called Beautiful, where he was put every day to beg from those going into the temple courts. [3]When he saw Peter and John about to enter, he asked them for money. [4]Peter looked straight at him, as did John. Then Peter said, "Look at us!" [5]So the man gave them his attention, expecting to get something from them.

[6]Then Peter said, "Silver or gold I do not have, but what I have I give you. In the name of Jesus Christ of Nazareth, walk." [7]Taking him by the right hand, he helped him up, and instantly the man's feet and ankles became strong. [8]He jumped to his feet and began to walk. Then he went with them into the temple courts, walking and jumping, and praising God. [9]When all the people saw him walking and praising God, [10]they recognized him as the same man who used to sit begging at the temple gate called Beautiful, and they were filled with wonder and amazement at what had happened to him.

REFLECT: 1. How is your church fellowship similar to and different from the fellowship described in these verses? How does this make you feel? 2. Do you think the fellowship described in this section can be duplicated today? Why or why not? Would you want a fellowship like that? Why or why not? If you did, what would you need to do to make it happen? 3. Of the fellowship's characteristics mentioned, which do you value most? Least? Why?

OPEN: When was the last time you jumped for joy? What happened?

DIG: 1. What do you think is the purpose of signs and miracles in the New Testament? In what way does the miracle in this passage fit this purpose? 2. Why does Peter emphasize that the man is healed "in the name of Jesus Christ of Nazareth"? How does this support your answers in question 1? 3. What is the result of this healing?

REFLECT: 1. What signs and wonders has God performed in your life? What was the result of these miracles? Why do you think God performed them? 2. How willing are you to let God work through you to bring others to him? What things prevent you from being more open to God's working through you? What will you do this week to overcome these hindrances?

[l]35 Psalm 110:1

Peter Speaks to the Onlookers

[11]While the beggar held on to Peter and John, all the people were astonished and came running to them in the place called Solomon's Colonnade. [12]When Peter saw this, he said to them: "Men of Israel, why does this surprise you? Why do you stare at us as if by our own power or godliness we had made this man walk? [13]The God of Abraham, Isaac and Jacob, the God of our fathers, has glorified his servant Jesus. You handed him over to be killed, and you disowned him before Pilate, though he had decided to let him go. [14]You disowned the Holy and Righteous One and asked that a murderer be released to you. [15]You killed the author of life, but God raised him from the dead. We are witnesses of this. [16]By faith in the name of Jesus, this man whom you see and know was made strong. It is Jesus' name and the faith that comes through him that has given this complete healing to him, as you can all see.

[17]"Now, brothers, I know that you acted in ignorance, as did your leaders. [18]But this is how God fulfilled what he had foretold through all the prophets, saying that his Christ[m] would suffer. [19]Repent, then, and turn to God, so that your sins may be wiped out, that times of refreshing may come from the Lord, [20]and that he may send the Christ, who has been appointed for you—even Jesus. [21]He must remain in heaven until the time comes for God to restore everything, as he promised long ago through his holy prophets. [22]For Moses said, 'The Lord your God will raise up for you a prophet like me from among your own people; you must listen to everything he tells you. [23]Anyone who does not listen to him will be completely cut off from among his people.'[n]

[24]"Indeed, all the prophets from Samuel on, as many as have spoken, have foretold these days. [25]And you are heirs of the prophets and of the covenant God made with your fathers. He said to Abraham, 'Through your offspring all peoples on earth will be blessed.'[o] [26]When God raised up his servant, he sent him first to you to bless you by turning each of you from your wicked ways."

Peter and John Before the Sanhedrin

4 The priests and the captain of the temple guard and the Sadducees came up to Peter and John while they were speaking to the people. [2]They were greatly disturbed because the apostles were teaching the people and proclaiming in Jesus the resurrection of the dead. [3]They seized Peter and John, and because it was evening, they put them in jail until the next day. [4]But many who heard the message believed, and the number of men grew to about five thousand.

[5]The next day the rulers, elders and teachers of the law met in Jerusalem. [6]Annas the high priest was there, and so were Caiaphas, John, Alexander and the other men of the high priest's family. [7]They had Peter and John brought before them and began to question them: "By what power or what name did you do this?"

[m]18 Or Messiah; also in verse 20   [n]23 Deut. 18:15,18,19   [o]25 Gen. 22:18; 26:4

[8]Then Peter, filled with the Holy Spirit, said to them: "Rulers and elders of the people! [9]If we are being called to account today for an act of kindness shown to a cripple and are asked how he was healed, [10]then know this, you and all the people of Israel: It is by the name of Jesus Christ of Nazareth, whom you crucified but whom God raised from the dead, that this man stands before you healed. [11]He is

" 'the stone you builders rejected,
    which has become the capstone.'[p][q]

[12]Salvation is found in no one else, for there is no other name under heaven given to men by which we must be saved."

[13]When they saw the courage of Peter and John and realized that they were unschooled, ordinary men, they were astonished and they took note that these men had been with Jesus. [14]But since they could see the man who had been healed standing there with them, there was nothing they could say. [15]So they ordered them to withdraw from the Sanhedrin and then conferred together. [16]"What are we going to do with these men?" they asked. "Everybody living in Jerusalem knows they have done an outstanding miracle, and we cannot deny it. [17]But to stop this thing from spreading any further among the people, we must warn these men to speak no longer to anyone in this name."

[18]Then they called them in again and commanded them not to speak or teach at all in the name of Jesus. [19]But Peter and John replied, "Judge for yourselves whether it is right in God's sight to obey you rather than God. [20]For we cannot help speaking about what we have seen and heard."

[21]After further threats they let them go. They could not decide how to punish them, because all the people were praising God for what had happened. [22]For the man who was miraculously healed was over forty years old.

The Believers' Prayer

[23]On their release, Peter and John went back to their own people and reported all that the chief priests and elders had said to them. [24]When they heard this, they raised their voices together in prayer to God. "Sovereign Lord," they said, "you made the heaven and the earth and the sea, and everything in them. [25]You spoke by the Holy Spirit through the mouth of your servant, our father David:

" 'Why do the nations rage
    and the peoples plot in vain?
[26]The kings of the earth take their stand
    and the rulers gather together
against the Lord
    and against his Anointed One.'[r][s]

[27]Indeed Herod and Pontius Pilate met together with the Gentiles and the people[t] of Israel in this city to conspire against your holy servant Jesus, whom you anointed. [28]They did what your

---

[p]11 Or *cornerstone*   [q]11 Psalm 118:22   [r]26 That is, Christ or Messiah
[s]26 Psalm 2:1,2   [t]27 The Greek is plural.

---

miracle, why do they want them to stop teaching? What does this tell you about their beliefs concerning Jesus? Why do you think they have these beliefs? **5.** What does verse 19 say about the religious leaders' relationship to God? How do you think this statement would be viewed by these leaders? By the people generally? Why? **6.** What is the effect of this hearing on the spread of the gospel? Why do you think it has so little effect?

REFLECT: 1. What is comforting to you about this story? Discomforting? Why? **2.** What's the most persecution you've ever experienced because of your faith? What happened? How did you handle it? **3.** How do you feel about civil disobedience? When, if ever, do you go against the authorities' commands? How do you accept the consequences? **4.** Do you think the prophesy in Luke 21: 12-19 applies to Christians today? Why or why not? Has God ever given you "words and wisdom" that nobody could refute? If so, what were the circumstances? How has this experience affected you? How bold are you in claiming this promise? What could you do to increase your boldness?

OPEN: When you were a child, who taught you the most about prayer? How?

DIG: 1. How have the opponents of Jesus, Peter, and John fulfilled David's prophecy in verses 25-26? Why do you think God used evil men and their intentions to fulfill his plans? **2.** How important is the role of prayer in the life of these believers? What is its effect on their witness? **3.** What is the role of the Holy Spirit in their witness? Without the Holy Spirit, how bold do you think they would have been?

REFLECT: 1. How are your prayers similar to and different from the prayer in this section? If God knows everything, why do these people tell him all the details (vv. 27-28)? What do you learn from this? **2.** If you were Peter or John, for what would you have asked after the encounter with the Jewish religious leaders, knowing that they had just crucified Jesus? Why? **3.** What inhibits you from letting the Holy Spirit make you bolder in your witness? What would need to happen for you to let go of this inhibition? What will you do this week to get rid of it?

REFLECT: **1.** What characterizes the believers in verses 32-34? How well would you have fit into the early church? What would have been most difficult for you to do? Why? **2.** How easy is it for you to share with others? What are the greatest barriers you face in being generous and open? **3.** To which needy person in your fellowship could you reach out this week? What will you do?

OPEN: What lie do you remember telling when you were a child? What happened?

DIG: **1.** Were Ananias and Sapphira required to sell the land and lay all the money at the apostles' feet? What was their sin? **2.** What would Ananias and Sapphira gain by lying about the money they received? How is your answer related to verses 32-37? **3.** Why do you think God punished them so severely? How would "great fear" be of use to God? How might it help the church?

REFLECT: **1.** If you had been one of the young men who buried Ananias and Sapphira, how do you think you'd have felt? Why? **2.** When have you been like Ananias and Sapphira and tried to fool God? What happened? What did you learn in that situation? How did God discipline you? How has your life changed since then? **3.** What do you learn about the fear of the Lord from this story? How will you apply this in your life today?

DIG: If the believers were highly regarded, why would no one join them in Solomon's Colonnade (see Acts 4:16-18)? Does this seem to have any effect on the growth of the church? Why do you think this is?

power and will had decided beforehand should happen. [29]Now, Lord, consider their threats and enable your servants to speak your word with great boldness. [30]Stretch out your hand to heal and perform miraculous signs and wonders through the name of your holy servant Jesus."

[31]After they prayed, the place where they were meeting was shaken. And they were all filled with the Holy Spirit and spoke the word of God boldly.

The Believers Share Their Possessions

[32]All the believers were one in heart and mind. No one claimed that any of his possessions was his own, but they shared everything they had. [33]With great power the apostles continued to testify to the resurrection of the Lord Jesus, and much grace was upon them all. [34]There were no needy persons among them. For from time to time those who owned lands or houses sold them, brought the money from the sales [35]and put it at the apostles' feet, and it was distributed to anyone as he had need.

[36]Joseph, a Levite from Cyprus, whom the apostles called Barnabas (which means Son of Encouragement), [37]sold a field he owned and brought the money and put it at the apostles' feet.

Ananias and Sapphira

5 Now a man named Ananias, together with his wife Sapphira, also sold a piece of property. [2]With his wife's full knowledge he kept back part of the money for himself, but brought the rest and put it at the apostles' feet.

[3]Then Peter said, "Ananias, how is it that Satan has so filled your heart that you have lied to the Holy Spirit and have kept for yourself some of the money you received for the land? [4]Didn't it belong to you before it was sold? And after it was sold, wasn't the money at your disposal? What made you think of doing such a thing? You have not lied to men but to God."

[5]When Ananias heard this, he fell down and died. And great fear seized all who heard what had happened. [6]Then the young men came forward, wrapped up his body, and carried him out and buried him.

[7]About three hours later his wife came in, not knowing what had happened. [8]Peter asked her, "Tell me, is this the price you and Ananias got for the land?"

"Yes," she said, "that is the price."

[9]Peter said to her, "How could you agree to test the Spirit of the Lord? Look! The feet of the men who buried your husband are at the door, and they will carry you out also."

[10]At that moment she fell down at his feet and died. Then the young men came in and, finding her dead, carried her out and buried her beside her husband. [11]Great fear seized the whole church and all who heard about these events.

The Apostles Heal Many

[12]The apostles performed many miraculous signs and wonders among the people. And all the believers used to meet together in Solomon's Colonnade. [13]No one else dared join them, even though they were highly regarded by the people.

[14]Nevertheless, more and more men and women believed in the Lord and were added to their number. [15]As a result, people brought the sick into the streets and laid them on beds and mats so that at least Peter's shadow might fall on some of them as he passed by. [16]Crowds gathered also from the towns around Jerusalem, bringing their sick and those tormented by evil[u] spirits, and all of them were healed.

The Apostles Persecuted

[17]Then the high priest and all his associates, who were members of the party of the Sadducees, were filled with jealousy. [18]They arrested the apostles and put them in the public jail. [19]But during the night an angel of the Lord opened the doors of the jail and brought them out. [20]"Go, stand in the temple courts," he said, "and tell the people the full message of this new life."

[21]At daybreak they entered the temple courts, as they had been told, and began to teach the people.

When the high priest and his associates arrived, they called together the Sanhedrin—the full assembly of the elders of Israel—and sent to the jail for the apostles. [22]But on arriving at the jail, the officers did not find them there. So they went back and reported, [23]"We found the jail securely locked, with the guards standing at the doors; but when we opened them, we found no one inside." [24]On hearing this report, the captain of the temple guard and the chief priests were puzzled, wondering what would come of this.

[25]Then someone came and said, "Look! The men you put in jail are standing in the temple courts teaching the people." [26]At that, the captain went with his officers and brought the apostles. They did not use force, because they feared that the people would stone them.

[27]Having brought the apostles, they made them appear before the Sanhedrin to be questioned by the high priest. [28]"We gave you strict orders not to teach in this name," he said. "Yet you have filled Jerusalem with your teaching and are determined to make us guilty of this man's blood."

[29]Peter and the other apostles replied: "We must obey God rather than men! [30]The God of our fathers raised Jesus from the dead—whom you had killed by hanging him on a tree. [31]God exalted him to his own right hand as Prince and Savior that he might give repentance and forgiveness of sins to Israel. [32]We are witnesses of these things, and so is the Holy Spirit, whom God has given to those who obey him."

[33]When they heard this, they were furious and wanted to put them to death. [34]But a Pharisee named Gamaliel, a teacher of the law, who was honored by all the people, stood up in the Sanhedrin and ordered that the men be put outside for a little while. [35]Then he addressed them: "Men of Israel, consider carefully what you intend to do to these men. [36]Some time ago Theudas appeared, claiming to be somebody, and about four hundred men rallied to him. He was killed, all his followers were dis-

[u]16 Greek *unclean*

REFLECT: Outside the church, how often do you get together with other believers? Where? How is this helpful? How necessary is Christian fellowship to you? Why?

OPEN: What's been one of the most miraculous deliverances you've ever experienced (from death, an illness, a bad habit, etc.)? How did it happen?

DIG: 1. What has made the Sadducees jealous? Why would this make them jealous? **2.** Why would God free the apostles and then risk their arrest again by sending them back to the temple to teach? What does their teaching accomplish? How does this support your answer about God's plan? **3.** How much courage would it take to return to the temple? Where do the apostles get this courage? What does this tell you about them? **4.** How would the apostles' teaching make the religious leaders guilty of Jesus' blood (v. 28)? If the people came to believe that they were guilty in this matter, what would happen to the religious leaders' authority? How does this relate to their concern over the teaching of the apostles? **5.** What does the apostles' answer in verse 29 tell you about their view of the religious leaders' authority? Would this be likely to decrease the tension between the two groups? Why or why not? What does this statement say about God's authority in the believer's life? **6.** In one sentence, what is the basic message of Gamaliel's speech? How does this relate to the apostles' statement in verse 29? Why does Gamaliel's speech calm the leaders when Peter's inflamed them? **7.** Why do you think the apostles rejoiced that they had been flogged? Why didn't this prevent them from teaching? What does this tell you about them?

REFLECT: 1. How do you think you would feel if you were sent to jail for what you believe? How would your family feel? What would this do to your life? **2.** What kind of disgrace have you suffered because you follow Jesus? Whom do you know who has been persecuted for his or her faith? What have you learned from this persecution? **3.** From what jail does the angel of the Lord need to free you so that you can proclaim Christ? **4.** What is the ultimate authority in your life? When does this create problems for you? What can you do to overcome these problems? **5.** When have you rejoiced in suffering? What made this particular suffering joyous? How does this relate to your ultimate authority?

DIG: **1.** What do you think has caused the problem in verse 1? How does the decision of the Twelve solve the problem without slowing growth? What does this tell you about their priorities? **2.** Do you think the disciples view this as a serious assignment for these seven men? Why or why not? **3.** Review quickly what has happened so far in Acts. How would you summarize what has happened so far? How does your summary compare with the summary in verse 7?

REFLECT: **1.** What's the most pressing problem facing your local church today? What are you doing to help solve the problem? **2.** What do you think is the biggest problem facing the church at large today? Why? What can you be doing about it?

OPEN: What was the worst lie anybody ever told about you? What made it the worst? Why do you think this person lied about you? How do you feel about this person today?

DIG: **1.** What impression do you get of Stephen in this passage? How is this related to the strategy his opponents use in verse 11? **2.** How are the charges against Stephen true? How are they false? What does this say about their understanding of Stephen's message?

REFLECT: **1.** In what ways is the description of Stephen in verses 8 and 10 a description of you? Which of Stephen's qualities do you feel you most need? Why

persed, and it all came to nothing. [37]After him, Judas the Galilean appeared in the days of the census and led a band of people in revolt. He too was killed, and all his followers were scattered. [38]Therefore, in the present case I advise you: Leave these men alone! Let them go! For if their purpose or activity is of human origin, it will fail. [39]But if it is from God, you will not be able to stop these men; you will only find yourselves fighting against God.''

[40]His speech persuaded them. They called the apostles in and had them flogged. Then they ordered them not to speak in the name of Jesus, and let them go.

[41]The apostles left the Sanhedrin, rejoicing because they had been counted worthy of suffering disgrace for the Name. [42]Day after day, in the temple courts and from house to house, they never stopped teaching and proclaiming the good news that Jesus is the Christ. [v]

The Choosing of the Seven

6 In those days when the number of disciples was increasing, the Grecian Jews among them complained against the Hebraic Jews because their widows were being overlooked in the daily distribution of food. [2]So the Twelve gathered all the disciples together and said, "It would not be right for us to neglect the ministry of the word of God in order to wait on tables. [3]Brothers, choose seven men from among you who are known to be full of the Spirit and wisdom. We will turn this responsibility over to them [4]and will give our attention to prayer and the ministry of the word."

[5]This proposal pleased the whole group. They chose Stephen, a man full of faith and of the Holy Spirit; also Philip, Procorus, Nicanor, Timon, Parmenas, and Nicolas from Antioch, a convert to Judaism. [6]They presented these men to the apostles, who prayed and laid their hands on them.

[7]So the word of God spread. The number of disciples in Jerusalem increased rapidly, and a large number of priests became obedient to the faith.

Stephen Seized

[8]Now Stephen, a man full of God's grace and power, did great wonders and miraculous signs among the people. [9]Opposition arose, however, from members of the Synagogue of the Freedmen (as it was called)—Jews of Cyrene and Alexandria as well as the provinces of Cilicia and Asia. These men began to argue with Stephen, [10]but they could not stand up against his wisdom or the Spirit by whom he spoke.

[11]Then they secretly persuaded some men to say, "We have heard Stephen speak words of blasphemy against Moses and against God."

[12]So they stirred up the people and the elders and the teachers of the law. They seized Stephen and brought him before the Sanhedrin. [13]They produced false witnesses, who testified, "This fellow never stops speaking against this holy place and

[v]42 Or Messiah   [w]3 Gen. 12:1   [x]7 Gen. 15:13,14

against the law. [14]For we have heard him say that this Jesus of Nazareth will destroy this place and change the customs Moses handed down to us."

[15]All who were sitting in the Sanhedrin looked intently at Stephen, and they saw that his face was like the face of an angel.

Stephen's Speech to the Sanhedrin

7 Then the high priest asked him, "Are these charges true?" [2]To this he replied: "Brothers and fathers, listen to me! The God of glory appeared to our father Abraham while he was still in Mesopotamia, before he lived in Haran. [3]'Leave your country and your people,' God said, 'and go to the land I will show you.'[w]

[4]"So he left the land of the Chaldeans and settled in Haran. After the death of his father, God sent him to this land where you are now living. [5]He gave him no inheritance here, not even a foot of ground. But God promised him that he and his descendants after him would possess the land, even though at that time Abraham had no child. [6]God spoke to him in this way: 'Your descendants will be strangers in a country not their own, and they will be enslaved and mistreated four hundred years. [7]But I will punish the nation they serve as slaves,' God said, 'and afterward they will come out of that country and worship me in this place.'[x] [8]Then he gave Abraham the covenant of circumcision. And Abraham became the father of Isaac and circumcised him eight days after his birth. Later Isaac became the father of Jacob, and Jacob became the father of the twelve patriarchs.

[9]"Because the patriarchs were jealous of Joseph, they sold him as a slave into Egypt. But God was with him [10]and rescued him from all his troubles. He gave Joseph wisdom and enabled him to gain the goodwill of Pharaoh king of Egypt; so he made him ruler over Egypt and all his palace.

[11]"Then a famine struck all Egypt and Canaan, bringing great suffering, and our fathers could not find food. [12]When Jacob heard that there was grain in Egypt, he sent our fathers on their first visit. [13]On their second visit, Joseph told his brothers who he was, and Pharaoh learned about Joseph's family. [14]After this, Joseph sent for his father Jacob and his whole family, seventy-five in all. [15]Then Jacob went down to Egypt, where he and our fathers died. [16]Their bodies were brought back to Shechem and placed in the tomb that Abraham had bought from the sons of Hamor at Shechem for a certain sum of money.

[17]"As the time drew near for God to fulfill his promise to Abraham, the number of our people in Egypt greatly increased. [18]Then another king, who knew nothing about Joseph, became ruler of Egypt. [19]He dealt treacherously with our people and oppressed our forefathers by forcing them to throw out their newborn babies so that they would die.

[20]"At that time Moses was born, and he was no ordinary child.[y] For three months he was cared for in his father's house. [21]When he was placed outside, Pharaoh's daughter took him and brought him up as her own son. [22]Moses was educated in all the wisdom of the Egyptians and was powerful in speech and action.

---

this one? What can you do this week to acquire this quality? **2.** How do you handle your opponents? What does this say about you?

OPEN: Who was the best storyteller you ever heard as a child? What made that person so effective?

DIG: 1. What does the high priest ask? From reading verses 1-52, what do you think Stephen's answer is? **2.** On what does Stephen base his defense? Why do you think he chose this as the basis of his defense? **3.** Who are the main characters of verses 2-48? How do each of these fit into God's plan? What is Stephen's main point in mentioning each of them? **4.** On which of these Old Testament characters does Stephen's defense concentrate most heavily? Why do you think he concentrates on this one? What does this tell you about the importance of this individual? How does this concentration relate to the charges brought against Stephen in Acts 6:13-14? **5.** What is Stephen's point in verses 48-50? How is this related to the charges against Stephen in Acts 6:13-14? **6.** Who is the prophet in verse 37? How does Stephen use the people's rejection of Moses in verse 39 to set up the high priest and the Sanhedrin? **7.** What is Stephen's accusation in verses 51-53? How does this relate to the previous fifty verses?

REFLECT: 1. Where is your Mesopotamia—the place where God's glory first appeared to you? How did it appear? **2.** In the past month, how have you felt "sent" by God? Where specifically has he sent you? What happened there? How did you know you were sent? **3.** Whose life do you think would have been hardest for you to live—Abraham's, Joseph's, or Moses'? Why? What do you learn about God's calling and the difficulties this can bring from reading about the lives of these men and Stephen? **4.** Who are some of the heroes (historical and contemporary) in your spiritual life? How did each influence you? How did you respond to them at first? Now? **5.** In what area do you most consistently resist the Holy Spirit? How does this compare to the resistance of the Sanhedrin (vv. 51-53)? How serious do you consider this problem?

---

y20 Or was fair in the sight of God

What would you need to do to overcome it? How will you begin today?

[23]"When Moses was forty years old, he decided to visit his fellow Israelites. [24]He saw one of them being mistreated by an Egyptian, so he went to his defense and avenged him by killing the Egyptian. [25]Moses thought that his own people would realize that God was using him to rescue them, but they did not. [26]The next day Moses came upon two Israelites who were fighting. He tried to reconcile them by saying, 'Men, you are brothers; why do you want to hurt each other?'

[27]"But the man who was mistreating the other pushed Moses aside and said, 'Who made you ruler and judge over us? [28]Do you want to kill me as you killed the Egyptian yesterday?'[z] [29]When Moses heard this, he fled to Midian, where he settled as a foreigner and had two sons.

[30]"After forty years had passed, an angel appeared to Moses in the flames of a burning bush in the desert near Mount Sinai. [31]When he saw this, he was amazed at the sight. As he went over to look more closely, he heard the Lord's voice: [32]'I am the God of your fathers, the God of Abraham, Isaac and Jacob.'[a] Moses trembled with fear and did not dare to look.

[33]"Then the Lord said to him, 'Take off your sandals; the place where you are standing is holy ground. [34]I have indeed seen the oppression of my people in Egypt. I have heard their groaning and have come down to set them free. Now come, I will send you back to Egypt.'[b]

[35]"This is the same Moses whom they had rejected with the words, 'Who made you ruler and judge?' He was sent to be their ruler and deliverer by God himself, through the angel who appeared to him in the bush. [36]He led them out of Egypt and did wonders and miraculous signs in Egypt, at the Red Sea[c] and for forty years in the desert.

[37]This is that Moses who told the Israelites, 'God will send you a prophet like me from your own people.'[d] [38]He was in the assembly in the desert, with the angel who spoke to him on Mount Sinai, and with our fathers; and he received living words to pass on to us.

[39]"But our fathers refused to obey him. Instead, they rejected him and in their hearts turned back to Egypt. [40]They told Aaron, 'Make us gods who will go before us. As for this fellow Moses who led us out of Egypt—we don't know what has happened to him!'[e] [41]That was the time they made an idol in the form of a calf. They brought sacrifices to it and held a celebration in honor of what their hands had made. [42]But God turned away and gave them over to the worship of the heavenly bodies. This agrees with what is written in the book of the prophets:

" 'Did you bring me sacrifices and offerings
forty years in the desert, O house of Israel?
[43]You have lifted up the shrine of Molech
and the star of your god Rephan,
the idols you made to worship.
Therefore I will send you into exile'[f] beyond Babylon.

---

[z]28 Exodus 2:14   [a]32 Exodus 3:6   [b]34 Exodus 3:5,7,8,10
[c]36 That is, Sea of Reeds   [d]37 Deut. 18:15   [e]40 Exodus 32:1
[f]43 Amos 5:25-27

44"Our forefathers had the tabernacle of the Testimony with them in the desert. It had been made as God directed Moses, according to the pattern he had seen. 45Having received the tabernacle, our fathers under Joshua brought it with them when they took the land from the nations God drove out before them. It remained in the land until the time of David, 46who enjoyed God's favor and asked that he might provide a dwelling place for the God of Jacob.*g* 47But it was Solomon who built the house for him.

48"However, the Most High does not live in houses made by men. As the prophet says:

49" 'Heaven is my throne,
    and the earth is my footstool.
What kind of house will you build for me?
                                    says the Lord.
Or where will my resting place be?
50Has not my hand made all these things?'*h*

51"You stiff-necked people, with uncircumcised hearts and ears! You are just like your fathers: You always resist the Holy Spirit! 52Was there ever a prophet your fathers did not persecute? They even killed those who predicted the coming of the Righteous One. And now you have betrayed and murdered him— 53you who have received the law that was put into effect through angels but have not obeyed it."

The Stoning of Stephen

54When they heard this, they were furious and gnashed their teeth at him. 55But Stephen, full of the Holy Spirit, looked up to heaven and saw the glory of God, and Jesus standing at the right hand of God. 56"Look," he said, "I see heaven open and the Son of Man standing at the right hand of God."

57At this they covered their ears and, yelling at the top of their voices, they all rushed at him, 58dragged him out of the city and began to stone him. Meanwhile, the witnesses laid their clothes at the feet of a young man named Saul.

59While they were stoning him, Stephen prayed, "Lord Jesus, receive my spirit." 60Then he fell on his knees and cried out, "Lord, do not hold this sin against them." When he had said this, he fell asleep.

8 And Saul was there, giving approval to his death.

The Church Persecuted and Scattered

On that day a great persecution broke out against the church at Jerusalem, and all except the apostles were scattered throughout Judea and Samaria. 2Godly men buried Stephen and mourned deeply for him. 3But Saul began to destroy the church. Going from house to house, he dragged off men and women and put them in prison.

DIG: 1. Why would Stephen's speech make the Sanhedrin angry? Why would Stephen's words in verse 56 make them murderous? 2. What do you learn about Stephen in verse 60? 3. Where was Saul from (see Acts 21:39)? How does this relate to Acts 6:9? What part do you think Saul played in the trial and execution of Stephen?

REFLECT: 1. What do you think was the secret of Stephen's ability to face persecution with a forgiving heart? How does this encourage you? 2. What's been the toughest test you've faced in the past year? How did God enable you to survive it? What did you learn?

DIG: 1. How might the scattering of the believers be good for the church? 2. What is Saul's aim? What are his actions? How do you think God is using this evil for good?

REFLECT: What is the worst thing that ever happened to you? How did God use it later for good in your life? What did you learn about God from this situation?

g46 Some early manuscripts the house of Jacob   *h50 Isaiah 66:1,2*

DIG: How does this passage relate to Acts 1:8? Why do you think God allowed the persecution of the Jerusalem church?

REFLECT: When has God had to force you out of the nest to get you to share your faith more effectively? What happened?

OPEN: Who is the most charismatic Christian you've ever known? How has this person influenced you?

DIG: **1**. What do Simon and Philip have in common (vv. 9-11)? How are they different? How has the crowd responded to both men in the past (vv. 6, 10-11)? **2**. What is the traditional relationship between the Jews and the Samaritans? Is it surprising that the Jerusalem church would send Peter and John to Samaria? What does this tell you about the importance of this mission? **3**. What is significant about receiving the Holy Spirit? What is especially significant about the Samaritans receiving the Holy Spirit? **4**. How sincere do you think Simon was about his commitment to Christ? What seems to be his motivation? **5**. What does Peter's rebuke in verses 20-23 tell you about Simon and his motivations? Do you think Simon's words in verse 24 reveal a change in his heart? Why or why not?

REFLECT: **1**. What was your primary motivation in receiving Jesus Christ as your Savior? What's your primary motivation in continuing in the faith? **2**. Has your personal influence declined or increased since you became a Christian? How? Why? **3**. In what ways do you identify with Simon in this passage? How will you incorporate this into your life this week?

OPEN: What is your most favorite road to travel? Your least favorite? Why?

DIG: **1**. Why would an Ethiopian have gone to Jerusalem to worship? How might this have prepared him to receive the gospel? **2**. What passage was the Ethiopian reading? Of whom is this passage speaking? Why would this pas-

Philip in Samaria

⁴Those who had been scattered preached the word wherever they went. ⁵Philip went down to a city in Samaria and proclaimed the Christ¹ there. ⁶When the crowds heard Philip and saw the miraculous signs he did, they all paid close attention to what he said. ⁷With shrieks, evil ʲ spirits came out of many, and many paralytics and cripples were healed. ⁸So there was great joy in that city.

Simon the Sorcerer

⁹Now for some time a man named Simon had practiced sorcery in the city and amazed all the people of Samaria. He boasted that he was someone great, ¹⁰and all the people, both high and low, gave him their attention and exclaimed, "This man is the divine power known as the Great Power." ¹¹They followed him because he had amazed them for a long time with his magic. ¹²But when they believed Philip as he preached the good news of the kingdom of God and the name of Jesus Christ, they were baptized, both men and women. ¹³Simon himself believed and was baptized. And he followed Philip everywhere, astonished by the great signs and miracles he saw.

¹⁴When the apostles in Jerusalem heard that Samaria had accepted the word of God, they sent Peter and John to them. ¹⁵When they arrived, they prayed for them that they might receive the Holy Spirit, ¹⁶because the Holy Spirit had not yet come upon any of them; they had simply been baptized into ᵏ the name of the Lord Jesus. ¹⁷Then Peter and John placed their hands on them, and they received the Holy Spirit.

¹⁸When Simon saw that the Spirit was given at the laying on of the apostles' hands, he offered them money ¹⁹and said, "Give me also this ability so that everyone on whom I lay my hands may receive the Holy Spirit."

²⁰Peter answered: "May your money perish with you, because you thought you could buy the gift of God with money! ²¹You have no part or share in this ministry, because your heart is not right before God. ²²Repent of this wickedness and pray to the Lord. Perhaps he will forgive you for having such a thought in your heart. ²³For I see that you are full of bitterness and captive to sin."

²⁴Then Simon answered, "Pray to the Lord for me so that nothing you have said may happen to me."

²⁵When they had testified and proclaimed the word of the Lord, Peter and John returned to Jerusalem, preaching the gospel in many Samaritan villages.

Philip and the Ethiopian

²⁶Now an angel of the Lord said to Philip, "Go south to the road—the desert road—that goes down from Jerusalem to Gaza." ²⁷So he started out, and on his way he met an Ethiopian ˡ eunuch, an important official in charge of all the treasury of Candace, queen of the Ethiopians. This man had gone to Jerusa-

---

ⁱ5 Or *Messiah*   ʲ7 Greek *unclean*   ᵏ16 Or *in*   ˡ27 That is, from the upper Nile region

lem to worship, [28]and on his way home was sitting in his chariot reading the book of Isaiah the prophet. [29]The Spirit told Philip, "Go to that chariot and stay near it."

[30]Then Philip ran up to the chariot and heard the man reading Isaiah the prophet. "Do you understand what you are reading?" Philip asked.

[31]"How can I," he said, "unless someone explains it to me?" So he invited Philip to come up and sit with him.

[32]The eunuch was reading this passage of Scripture:

"He was led like a sheep to the slaughter,
and as a lamb before the shearer is silent,
so he did not open his mouth.
[33]In his humiliation he was deprived of justice.
Who can speak of his descendants?
For his life was taken from the earth."[m]

[34]The eunuch asked Philip, "Tell me, please, who is the prophet talking about, himself or someone else?" [35]Then Philip began with that very passage of Scripture and told him the good news about Jesus.

[36]As they traveled along the road, they came to some water and the eunuch said, "Look, here is water. Why shouldn't I be baptized?"[n] [38]And he gave orders to stop the chariot. Then both Philip and the eunuch went down into the water and Philip baptized him. [39]When they came up out of the water, the Spirit of the Lord suddenly took Philip away, and the eunuch did not see him again, but went on his way rejoicing. [40]Philip, however, appeared at Azotus and traveled about, preaching the gospel in all the towns until he reached Caesarea.

Saul's Conversion

[9] Meanwhile, Saul was still breathing out murderous threats against the Lord's disciples. He went to the high priest [2]and asked him for letters to the synagogues in Damascus, so that if he found any there who belonged to the Way, whether men or women, he might take them as prisoners to Jerusalem. [3]As he neared Damascus on his journey, suddenly a light from heaven flashed around him. [4]He fell to the ground and heard a voice say to him, "Saul, Saul, why do you persecute me?"

[5]"Who are you, Lord?" Saul asked.

"I am Jesus, whom you are persecuting," he replied. [6]"Now get up and go into the city, and you will be told what you must do."

[7]The men traveling with Saul stood there speechless; they heard the sound but did not see anyone. [8]Saul got up from the ground, but when he opened his eyes he could see nothing. So they led him by the hand into Damascus. [9]For three days he was blind, and did not eat or drink anything.

[10]In Damascus there was a disciple named Ananias. The Lord called to him in a vision, "Ananias!"

"Yes, Lord," he answered.

---

[m]33 Isaiah 53:7,8   [n]36 Some late manuscripts baptized?" [37]Philip said, "If you believe with all your heart, you may." The eunuch answered, "I believe that Jesus Christ is the Son of God."

---

sage be especially appropriate for Philip's message to the Ethiopian? **3.** Why would Philip be especially qualified to relate the gospel to the Ethiopian? **4.** What does the baptism of the Ethiopian signify? **5.** Make a list of the things God did in this passage to prepare the way for his message. What is the relationship between this preparation and human initiative in this story? What does this teach you about how God operates through man?

REFLECT: 1. What has been your Gaza road—a place where you shared the good news in an unusual way? **2.** What role does God's preparation play in evangelism? In personal initiative? In meeting a person where he or she is? How is Philip's style of evangelism similar to yours? How is it different? **3.** What is one of your greatest barriers to sharing your faith? How do you think you could get past that barrier? **4.** How ready are you to initiate the action of witnessing? What does this say about your faith in God's preparation?

OPEN: If you knew you were losing your sight tomorrow, what would you want to see today? What does this tell you about yourself?

DIG: 1. Look up "Paul" in a Bible dictionary. What things do you find outstanding about Paul before his conversion? Who was Saul's famous teacher? What role has this teacher played in Acts to this point? Do his beliefs about the Christians seem to have had any effect on Saul? **2.** In verses 1-2, do you think Saul is sincere in his beliefs? What do you think motivates him? How deep would you say is his love for God? What makes you say this? **3.** Why do you think God would want to use a man like Saul? What character traits does Saul have that God could use? How might his past be helpful to God's plan to spread the gospel? **4.** Why do you think God used such dramatic means to get Saul's attention? What is significant about the three days of blindness for Saul? How do you think Saul felt for these three days? What do you think Saul learned from this whole experience? **5.** How hard would it be for Ananias to go to Saul? How willingly does he seem to go? What does it tell you about Ananias that he does go?

REFLECT: 1. Where has been your road to Damascus—the place where God first got your attention? How does Jesus usually get your attention now? **2.** Where is your Straight Street—the place where it's tough to obey the Lord? What makes this place so difficult for you? **3.** Who has been an Ananias in your life? What did that person do for you? To whom have you been an Ananias? How? **4.** Which of your character traits does God use to further his plans?

OPEN: When you were a teenager, who was your closest friend? How did the two of you defend and support each other?

DIG: 1. Which would you say characterizes Saul's approach—antagonism or gentle persuasion? Is this surprising to you? Why or why not? What is the effect of his preaching? **2.** What is ironic about verses 23-25? What would Saul learn from this experience? Why do you think God allowed this to happen to Saul? **3.** How do you think Saul felt when the disciples in Jerusalem were afraid of him? What do you learn about Barnabas' character in this passage? **4.** Look at a map to see how far the church has spread. How does this relate to Acts 1:8? What are the characteristics of the church at this point? How are each of these marks of a healthy spiritual life?

REFLECT: 1. When have you had to live down a reputation? What strategy did you use to do it? What did you learn in that situation? **2.** Who has been a Barnabas to you? How? To whom have you served as a Barnabas? **3.** Who are the brothers and sisters who are close to you spiritually? How have they supported you in the past? **4.** In what phase is your life now? How would you characterize it? How is it different from previous phases? How well do you like this time of your life? Why?

[11]The Lord told him, "Go to the house of Judas on Straight Street and ask for a man from Tarsus named Saul, for he is praying. [12]In a vision he has seen a man named Ananias come and place his hands on him to restore his sight."

[13]"Lord," Ananias answered, "I have heard many reports about this man and all the harm he has done to your saints in Jerusalem. [14]And he has come here with authority from the chief priests to arrest all who call on your name."

[15]But the Lord said to Ananias, "Go! This man is my chosen instrument to carry my name before the Gentiles and their kings and before the people of Israel. [16]I will show him how much he must suffer for my name."

[17]Then Ananias went to the house and entered it. Placing his hands on Saul, he said, "Brother Saul, the Lord—Jesus, who appeared to you on the road as you were coming here—has sent me so that you may see again and be filled with the Holy Spirit." [18]Immediately, something like scales fell from Saul's eyes, and he could see again. He got up and was baptized, [19]and after taking some food, he regained his strength.

Saul in Damascus and Jerusalem

Saul spent several days with the disciples in Damascus. [20]At once he began to preach in the synagogues that Jesus is the Son of God. [21]All those who heard him were astonished and asked, "Isn't he the man who raised havoc in Jerusalem among those who call on this name? And hasn't he come here to take them as prisoners to the chief priests?" [22]Yet Saul grew more and more powerful and baffled the Jews living in Damascus by proving that Jesus is the Christ.[o]

[23]After many days had gone by, the Jews conspired to kill him, [24]but Saul learned of their plan. Day and night they kept close watch on the city gates in order to kill him. [25]But his followers took him by night and lowered him in a basket through an opening in the wall.

[26]When he came to Jerusalem, he tried to join the disciples, but they were all afraid of him, not believing that he really was a disciple. [27]But Barnabas took him and brought him to the apostles. He told them how Saul on his journey had seen the Lord and that the Lord had spoken to him, and how in Damascus he had preached fearlessly in the name of Jesus. [28]So Saul stayed with them and moved about freely in Jerusalem, speaking boldly in the name of the Lord. [29]He talked and debated with the Grecian Jews, but they tried to kill him. [30]When the brothers learned of this, they took him down to Caesarea and sent him off to Tarsus.

[31]Then the church throughout Judea, Galilee and Samaria enjoyed a time of peace. It was strengthened; and encouraged by the Holy Spirit, it grew in numbers, living in the fear of the Lord.

o22 Or Messiah

Aeneas and Dorcas

[32]As Peter traveled about the country, he went to visit the saints in Lydda. [33]There he found a man named Aeneas, a paralytic who had been bedridden for eight years. [34]"Aeneas," Peter said to him, "Jesus Christ heals you. Get up and take care of your mat." Immediately Aeneas got up. [35]All those who lived in Lydda and Sharon saw him and turned to the Lord.

[36]In Joppa there was a disciple named Tabitha (which, when translated, is Dorcas[p]), who was always doing good and helping the poor. [37]About that time she became sick and died, and her body was washed and placed in an upstairs room. [38]Lydda was near Joppa; so when the disciples heard that Peter was in Lydda, they sent two men to him and urged him, "Please come at once!"

[39]Peter went with them, and when he arrived he was taken upstairs to the room. All the widows stood around him, crying and showing him the robes and other clothing that Dorcas had made while she was still with them.

[40]Peter sent them all out of the room; then he got down on his knees and prayed. Turning toward the dead woman, he said, "Tabitha, get up." She opened her eyes, and seeing Peter she sat up. [41]He took her by the hand and helped her to her feet. Then he called the believers and the widows and presented her to them alive. [42]This became known all over Joppa, and many people believed in the Lord. [43]Peter stayed in Joppa for some time with a tanner named Simon.

Cornelius Calls for Peter

10 At Caesarea there was a man named Cornelius, a centurion in what was known as the Italian Regiment. [2]He and all his family were devout and God-fearing; he gave generously to those in need and prayed to God regularly. [3]One day at about three in the afternoon he had a vision. He distinctly saw an angel of God, who came to him and said, "Cornelius!"

[4]Cornelius stared at him in fear. "What is it, Lord?" he asked.

The angel answered, "Your prayers and gifts to the poor have come up as a memorial offering before God. [5]Now send men to Joppa to bring back a man named Simon who is called Peter. [6]He is staying with Simon the tanner, whose house is by the sea."

[7]When the angel who spoke to him had gone, Cornelius called two of his servants and a devout soldier who was one of his attendants. [8]He told them everything that had happened and sent them to Joppa.

Peter's Vision

[9]About noon the following day as they were on their journey and approaching the city, Peter went up on the roof to pray. [10]He became hungry and wanted something to eat, and while the meal was being prepared, he fell into a trance. [11]He saw heaven opened and something like a large sheet being let down to earth by its four corners. [12]It contained all kinds of four-footed ani-

OPEN: What would you like people to say about you at your funeral? What statement would you liked etched on your tombstone?

DIG: 1. What is the result of Peter's visit for Aeneas and for Dorcas? What is the result of his visit for the towns of Lydda and Joppa? Which result is the most important? Why? What do you believe is the purpose of miracles in God's plan? **2.** What seems to be the key to the raising of Dorcas? How is this different from the healing of Aeneas? Why do you think there is a difference? What do you learn about God's power from these two miracles? **3.** Which of Jesus' miracles do these two incidents remind you of? How is Peter now like Jesus?

REFLECT: 1. How have you experienced God's healing in your life? What were the results of this healing for you? For others? What do you think was the purpose of this healing? **2.** When do you pray the most? Why? What are the strengths and weaknesses of your prayer life? What can you begin to do today to strengthen these weaknesses?

DIG: 1. What do you learn about Cornelius in verses 1-3? What do you know about the Italian Regiment? About being a centurion? **2.** How does his lifestyle affect God's attitude toward him? What does this say about the importance of lifestyle?

REFLECT: 1. If verses 1-3 were about you, what would they say? What does this say about your relationship with God? **2.** What is good about your lifestyle? What is bad about your lifestyle? How is your relationship with God affected by what is good about your lifestyle? By what is bad? What can you do this week to begin getting rid of the bad aspects of your lifestyle?

OPEN: How often do you daydream? What do you most often daydream about? Why?

DIG: 1. Look up Caesaria in a Bible dictionary. What is the political importance of this city in Peter's day? How would you describe its social character? What would this mean to a Jew like Peter? How likely would Peter be

[p]36 Both *Tabitha* (Aramaic) and *Dorcas* (Greek) mean *gazelle*.

to go to this city of his own free will? **2.** In Peter's vision, why does he refuse to eat? What new guiding principle does God give him in verse 15? What does this have to do with Caesaria? What are its practical implications for Peter's visit in a Gentile home? **3.** What does this passage tell you is of primary importance to Peter? What do you learn about Peter's relationship to God?

REFLECT: 1. How do you feel about visions and trances? Do you believe God speaks through dreams today? Why or why not? **2.** When, if ever, have you felt God speaking to you through a dream? What happened? **3.** What are some principles or beliefs of yours that God might need to modify? **4.** What new relationships has God given you recently? How has he brought these people into your life? How have you influenced each other?

OPEN: When was the first time you remember encountering prejudice? What do you remember about your feelings? How did this occurrence affect your life?

DIG: 1. How anxious does Cornelius appear to meet Peter? Does he seem to understand who Peter is? What does this say about his level of understanding concerning matters of salvation? **2.** How effective was the vision of verses 11-16 in changing Peter's attitudes toward Gentiles? Of what importance was this to Cornelius? What do you learn from this about God's concern for people honestly seeking him? **3.** Read verses 27-29 and 34-35. What do you learn from these verses about God's view of people? About his view of non-believers? **4.** Why do the Gentiles begin speaking in tongues? What is the importance of this to Peter and the other Jews? **5.** Summarize Peter's message to these people. **6.** How is Peter's message to Gentiles different from his approach to the Jews (2:36-41, 3:13-15)? What do you conclude from this? **7.** How did God remove the prejudices of both Peter and Cornelius? What part did obedience play in the removal of these prejudices?

mals, as well as reptiles of the earth and birds of the air. [13]Then a voice told him, "Get up, Peter. Kill and eat."

[14]"Surely not, Lord!" Peter replied. "I have never eaten anything impure or unclean."

[15]The voice spoke to him a second time, "Do not call anything impure that God has made clean."

[16]This happened three times, and immediately the sheet was taken back to heaven.

[17]While Peter was wondering about the meaning of the vision, the men sent by Cornelius found out where Simon's house was and stopped at the gate. [18]They called out, asking if Simon who was known as Peter was staying there.

[19]While Peter was still thinking about the vision, the Spirit said to him, "Simon, three[q] men are looking for you. [20]So get up and go downstairs. Do not hesitate to go with them, for I have sent them."

[21]Peter went down and said to the men, "I'm the one you're looking for. Why have you come?"

[22]The men replied, "We have come from Cornelius the centurion. He is a righteous and God-fearing man, who is respected by all the Jewish people. A holy angel told him to have you come to his house so that he could hear what you have to say." [23]Then Peter invited the men into the house to be his guests.

Peter at Cornelius' House

The next day Peter started out with them, and some of the brothers from Joppa went along. [24]The following day he arrived in Caesarea. Cornelius was expecting them and had called together his relatives and close friends. [25]As Peter entered the house, Cornelius met him and fell at his feet in reverence. [26]But Peter made him get up. "Stand up," he said, "I am only a man myself."

[27]Talking with him, Peter went inside and found a large gathering of people. [28]He said to them: "You are well aware that it is against our law for a Jew to associate with a Gentile or visit him. But God has shown me that I should not call any man impure or unclean. [29]So when I was sent for, I came without raising any objection. May I ask why you sent for me?"

[30]Cornelius answered: "Four days ago I was in my house praying at this hour, at three in the afternoon. Suddenly a man in shining clothes stood before me [31]and said, 'Cornelius, God has heard your prayer and remembered your gifts to the poor. [32]Send to Joppa for Simon who is called Peter. He is a guest in the home of Simon the tanner, who lives by the sea.' [33]So I sent for you immediately, and it was good of you to come. Now we are all here in the presence of God to listen to everything the Lord has commanded you to tell us."

[34]Then Peter began to speak: "I now realize how true it is that God does not show favoritism [35]but accepts men from every nation who fear him and do what is right. [36]You know the message God sent to the people of Israel, telling the good news of peace through Jesus Christ, who is Lord of all. [37]You know

---

q19 One early manuscript *two*; other manuscripts do not have the number.

what has happened throughout Judea, beginning in Galilee after the baptism that John preached— ³⁸how God anointed Jesus of Nazareth with the Holy Spirit and power, and how he went around doing good and healing all who were under the power of the devil, because God was with him.

³⁹"We are witnesses of everything he did in the country of the Jews and in Jerusalem. They killed him by hanging him on a tree, ⁴⁰but God raised him from the dead on the third day and caused him to be seen. ⁴¹He was not seen by all the people, but by witnesses whom God had already chosen—by us who ate and drank with him after he rose from the dead. ⁴²He commanded us to preach to the people and to testify that he is the one whom God appointed as judge of the living and the dead. ⁴³All the prophets testify about him that everyone who believes in him receives forgiveness of sins through his name."

⁴⁴While Peter was still speaking these words, the Holy Spirit came on all who heard the message. ⁴⁵The circumcised believers who had come with Peter were astonished that the gift of the Holy Spirit had been poured out even on the Gentiles. ⁴⁶For they heard them speaking in tongues^r and praising God.

Then Peter said, ⁴⁷"Can anyone keep these people from being baptized with water? They have received the Holy Spirit just as we have." ⁴⁸So he ordered that they be baptized in the name of Jesus Christ. Then they asked Peter to stay with them for a few days.

Peter Explains His Actions

11 The apostles and the brothers throughout Judea heard that the Gentiles also had received the word of God. ²So when Peter went up to Jerusalem, the circumcised believers criticized him ³and said, "You went into the house of uncircumcised men and ate with them."

⁴Peter began and explained everything to them precisely as it had happened: ⁵"I was in the city of Joppa praying, and in a trance I saw a vision. I saw something like a large sheet being let down from heaven by its four corners, and it came down to where I was. ⁶I looked into it and saw four-footed animals of the earth, wild beasts, reptiles, and birds of the air. ⁷Then I heard a voice telling me, 'Get up, Peter. Kill and eat.'

⁸"I replied, 'Surely not, Lord! Nothing impure or unclean has ever entered my mouth.'

⁹"The voice spoke from heaven a second time, 'Do not call anything impure that God has made clean.' ¹⁰This happened three times, and then it was all pulled up to heaven again.

¹¹"Right then three men who had been sent to me from Caesarea stopped at the house where I was staying. ¹²The Spirit told me to have no hesitation about going with them. These six brothers also went with me, and we entered the man's house. ¹³He told us how he had seen an angel appear in his house and say, 'Send to Joppa for Simon who is called Peter. ¹⁴He will bring you a message through which you and all your household will be saved.'

^r46 Or *other languages*

REFLECT: 1. How grateful are you toward pastors and teachers who convey God's truths to you? How do you express your gratitude? What could you do this week to communicate your gratitude? **2.** How important do you think it is to give to the poor? How do you give to the poor? How has this giving strengthened your relationship with Christ? **3.** How has the Peter-Cornelius relationship affected your life? If they had not met, what do you think would have happened to you? **4.** In what areas are you prejudiced? What do you think God wants to do with your prejudices? How has he overcome your prejudices in the past? **5.** What have you learned about evangelism from this passage? About obedience? How will you apply what you've learned?

OPEN: If you were a full-time missionary, where would you want to serve? Why? What would you want to be doing? Why?

DIG: 1. Why would the believers in Jerusalem be concerned that Peter had preached to the Gentiles? How do their concerns compare to Peter's in Acts 10:9-16? **2.** How do verses 5-10 compare with 16-17 and Ephesians 3:6? What do you learn from this comparison? **3.** Do you learn anything new from Peter's account that you did not learn in chapter 10? What do you conclude from reading this? **4.** How often does Peter refer to God, the Lord, Jesus, or the Holy Spirit? What's significant about this? **5.** Of what importance is the gift of the Holy Spirit in Peter's argument? Why would this argument have such a strong effect on the Jerusalem believers? **6.** Why do you think God chose Peter to be the first to go to the Gentiles? Do you think another disciple would have been as successful in both Caesaria and Jerusalem? Why or why not?

REFLECT: 1. What were you criticized for this week? How did you handle it? What did you learn from this experience? **2.** What type of persons do you think are discriminated against by the church today? Why this group? What principles can you apply from this passage in dealing with these people? How will you begin applying these principles this week?

OPEN: When, if ever, have you been in a natural disaster? What happened?

DIG: 1. What do you know about Phoenicia, Cyprus, and Antioch? How significant were these places to the culture of that time? 2. Why would men from Cyprus and Cyrene probably be effective with Greeks in Antioch? 3. What previous connection is there between Saul and Barnabas? Why do you think Barnabas uses Saul? How would this be a help to Saul? To the church? 4. What do you learn about the nature of the Antioch church when they send aid to the Jerusalem church?

REFLECT: 1. With which affinity groups could you share your faith? How does having a common bond help you in sharing the gospel? 2. How can you help younger Christians grow and develop this week?

OPEN: What was the most unbelievable news you ever heard? What did it take to convince you of its truth?

DIG: 1. Look up Herod Agrippa I in a Bible dictionary. What kind of a man was he? Why would he want to please the Jews? How would persecuting the Christians please the Jews? What significant change in attitude does this suggest (see Acts 4:21-22)? Why might this change have taken place? 2. What is the irony of the situation in verses 13-15? How much faith do the Jerusalem believers exhibit in their prayer? How do you explain this? How does this relate to verse 2? What part do you think prayer had in Peter's escape? Why? 3. Why do

[15]"As I began to speak, the Holy Spirit came on them as he had come on us at the beginning. [16]Then I remembered what the Lord had said: 'John baptized with[1] water, but you will be baptized with the Holy Spirit.' [17]So if God gave them the same gift as he gave us, who believed in the Lord Jesus Christ, who was I to think that I could oppose God?"

[18]When they heard this, they had no further objections and praised God, saying, "So then, God has granted even the Gentiles repentance unto life."

The Church in Antioch

[19]Now those who had been scattered by the persecution in connection with Stephen traveled as far as Phoenicia, Cyprus and Antioch, telling the message only to Jews. [20]Some of them, however, men from Cyprus and Cyrene, went to Antioch and began to speak to Greeks also, telling them the good news about the Lord Jesus. [21]The Lord's hand was with them, and a great number of people believed and turned to the Lord.

[22]News of this reached the ears of the church at Jerusalem, and they sent Barnabas to Antioch. [23]When he arrived and saw the evidence of the grace of God, he was glad and encouraged them all to remain true to the Lord with all their hearts. [24]He was a good man, full of the Holy Spirit and faith, and a great number of people were brought to the Lord.

[25]Then Barnabas went to Tarsus to look for Saul, [26]and when he found him, he brought him to Antioch. So for a whole year Barnabas and Saul met with the church and taught great numbers of people. The disciples were called Christians first at Antioch.

[27]During this time some prophets came down from Jerusalem to Antioch. [28]One of them, named Agabus, stood up and through the Spirit predicted that a severe famine would spread over the entire Roman world. (This happened during the reign of Claudius.) [29]The disciples, each according to his ability, decided to provide help for the brothers living in Judea. [30]This they did, sending their gift to the elders by Barnabas and Saul.

Peter's Miraculous Escape From Prison

12 It was about this time that King Herod arrested some who belonged to the church, intending to persecute them. [2]He had James, the brother of John, put to death with the sword. [3]When he saw that this pleased the Jews, he proceeded to seize Peter also. This happened during the Feast of Unleavened Bread. [4]After arresting him, he put him in prison, handing him over to be guarded by four squads of four soldiers each. Herod intended to bring him out for public trial after the Passover.

[5]So Peter was kept in prison, but the church was earnestly praying to God for him.

[6]The night before Herod was to bring him to trial, Peter was sleeping between two soldiers, bound with two chains, and sentries stood guard at the entrance. [7]Suddenly an angel of the

[1]16 Or *in*

Lord appeared and a light shone in the cell. He struck Peter on the side and woke him up. "Quick, get up!" he said, and the chains fell off Peter's wrists.

[8]Then the angel said to him, "Put on your clothes and sandals." And Peter did so. "Wrap your cloak around you and follow me," the angel told him. [9]Peter followed him out of the prison, but he had no idea that what the angel was doing was really happening; he thought he was seeing a vision. [10]They passed the first and second guards and came to the iron gate leading to the city. It opened for them by itself, and they went through it. When they had walked the length of one street, suddenly the angel left him.

[11]Then Peter came to himself and said, "Now I know without a doubt that the Lord sent his angel and rescued me from Herod's clutches and from everything the Jewish people were anticipating."

[12]When this had dawned on him, he went to the house of Mary the mother of John, also called Mark, where many people had gathered and were praying. [13]Peter knocked at the outer entrance, and a servant girl named Rhoda came to answer the door. [14]When she recognized Peter's voice, she was so overjoyed she ran back without opening it and exclaimed, "Peter is at the door!"

[15]"You're out of your mind," they told her. When she kept insisting that it was so, they said, "It must be his angel."

[16]But Peter kept on knocking, and when they opened the door and saw him, they were astonished. [17]Peter motioned with his hand for them to be quiet and described how the Lord had brought him out of prison. "Tell James and the brothers about this," he said, and then he left for another place.

[18]In the morning, there was no small commotion among the soldiers as to what had become of Peter. [19]After Herod had a thorough search made for him and did not find him, he cross-examined the guards and ordered that they be executed.

Herod's Death

Then Herod went from Judea to Caesarea and stayed there a while. [20]He had been quarreling with the people of Tyre and Sidon; they now joined together and sought an audience with him. Having secured the support of Blastus, a trusted personal servant of the king, they asked for peace, because they depended on the king's country for their food supply.

[21]On the appointed day Herod, wearing his royal robes, sat on his throne and delivered a public address to the people. [22]They shouted, "This is the voice of a god, not of a man." [23]Immediately, because Herod did not give praise to God, an angel of the Lord struck him down, and he was eaten by worms and died.

[24]But the word of God continued to increase and spread.

[25]When Barnabas and Saul had finished their mission, they returned from[t] Jerusalem, taking with them John, also called Mark.

[t]25 Some manuscripts *to*

you think God miraculously freed Peter? What does this say about the importance of Peter to the church? 4. Who is the James of verse 17 (see Gal. 1:18-19)? Why do you think he is mentioned specifically? What does this tell you about his importance in the Jerusalem church?

REFLECT: 1. What is one "jail" God has liberated you from? How did he do it? How aware were you that it was happening at the time? 2. How are you like the people at the prayer meeting in this story? What are some of your prayers that you'd be surprised if God answered? Why? 3. What do you think would happen to your faith if one of your closest friends were murdered by the government because he believed in Jesus? Do you think you'd be less vocal? Hold your meetings in secret? Why? 4. Have you ever had people who supported you turn against you because of your faith? What were the circumstances? Did this increase or decrease your faith? Why? What was God's response to this problem? How will his response help you in the future?

OPEN: Whom would you nominate as the All-Time Worst Government Official? Why?

DIG: 1. Why do you think the author included this episode here? How permanent was Herod's power over the Christians? How does this contrast to his power over the church in verse 24? 2. Review quickly the different persecutions faced by the church so far in Acts. In the face of all these persecutions, what is the importance of verse 24? What does it say about the power of truth?

REFLECT: When does your faith seem like weakness to you? How does this relate to the events of this chapter? What will you do to change this attitude to one of strength and confidence?

Barnabas and Saul Sent Off

13 In the church at Antioch there were prophets and teachers: Barnabas, Simeon called Niger, Lucius of Cyrene, Manaen (who had been brought up with Herod the tetrarch) and Saul. ²While they were worshiping the Lord and fasting, the Holy Spirit said, "Set apart for me Barnabas and Saul for the work to which I have called them." ³So after they had fasted and prayed, they placed their hands on them and sent them off.

On Cyprus

⁴The two of them, sent on their way by the Holy Spirit, went down to Seleucia and sailed from there to Cyprus. ⁵When they arrived at Salamis, they proclaimed the word of God in the Jewish synagogues. John was with them as their helper.

⁶They traveled through the whole island until they came to Paphos. There they met a Jewish sorcerer and false prophet named Bar-Jesus, ⁷who was an attendant of the proconsul, Sergius Paulus. The proconsul, an intelligent man, sent for Barnabas and Saul because he wanted to hear the word of God. ⁸But Elymas the sorcerer (for that is what his name means) opposed them and tried to turn the proconsul from the faith. ⁹Then Saul, who was also called Paul, filled with the Holy Spirit, looked straight at Elymas and said, ¹⁰"You are a child of the devil and an enemy of everything that is right! You are full of all kinds of deceit and trickery. Will you never stop perverting the right ways of the Lord? ¹¹Now the hand of the Lord is against you. You are going to be blind, and for a time you will be unable to see the light of the sun."

Immediately mist and darkness came over him, and he groped about, seeking someone to lead him by the hand. ¹²When the proconsul saw what had happened, he believed, for he was amazed at the teaching about the Lord.

In Pisidian Antioch

¹³From Paphos, Paul and his companions sailed to Perga in Pamphylia, where John left them to return to Jerusalem. ¹⁴From Perga they went on to Pisidian Antioch. On the Sabbath they entered the synagogue and sat down. ¹⁵After the reading from the Law and the Prophets, the synagogue rulers sent word to them, saying, "Brothers, if you have a message of encouragement for the people, please speak."

¹⁶Standing up, Paul motioned with his hand and said: "Men of Israel and you Gentiles who worship God, listen to me! ¹⁷The God of the people of Israel chose our fathers; he made the people prosper during their stay in Egypt, with mighty power he led them out of that country, ¹⁸he endured their conduct ᵘ for about forty years in the desert, ¹⁹he overthrew seven nations in Canaan and gave their land to his people as their inheritance. ²⁰All this took about 450 years.

"After this, God gave them judges until the time of Samuel the prophet. ²¹Then the people asked for a king, and he gave them Saul son of Kish, of the tribe of Benjamin, who ruled forty

ᵘ*18 Some manuscripts and cared for them*

years. ²²After removing Saul, he made David their king. He testified concerning him: 'I have found David son of Jesse a man after my own heart; he will do everything I want him to do.'

²³"From this man's descendants God has brought to Israel the Savior Jesus, as he promised. ²⁴Before the coming of Jesus, John preached repentance and baptism to all the people of Israel. ²⁵As John was completing his work, he said: 'Who do you think I am? I am not that one. No, but he is coming after me, whose sandals I am not worthy to untie.'

²⁶"Brothers, children of Abraham, and you God-fearing Gentiles, it is to us that this message of salvation has been sent. ²⁷The people of Jerusalem and their rulers did not recognize Jesus, yet in condemning him they fulfilled the words of the prophets that are read every Sabbath. ²⁸Though they found no proper ground for a death sentence, they asked Pilate to have him executed. ²⁹When they had carried out all that was written about him, they took him down from the tree and laid him in a tomb. ³⁰But God raised him from the dead, ³¹and for many days he was seen by those who had traveled with him from Galilee to Jerusalem. They are now his witnesses to our people.

³²"We tell you the good news: What God promised our fathers ³³he has fulfilled for us, their children, by raising up Jesus. As it is written in the second Psalm:

" 'You are my Son;
    today I have become your Father.'ᵛ ʷ

³⁴The fact that God raised him from the dead, never to decay, is stated in these words:

" 'I will give you the holy and sure blessings promised
    to David.'ˣ

³⁵So it is stated elsewhere:

" 'You will not let your Holy One see decay.'ʸ

³⁶"For when David had served God's purpose in his own generation, he fell asleep; he was buried with his fathers and his body decayed. ³⁷But the one whom God raised from the dead did not see decay.

³⁸"Therefore, my brothers, I want you to know that through Jesus the forgiveness of sins is proclaimed to you. ³⁹Through him everyone who believes is justified from everything you could not be justified from by the law of Moses. ⁴⁰Take care that what the prophets have said does not happen to you:

⁴¹" 'Look, you scoffers,
    wonder and perish,
for I am going to do something in your days
    that you would never believe,
    even if someone told you.'ᶻ"

⁴²As Paul and Barnabas were leaving the synagogue, the people invited them to speak further about these things on the the church? **6.** What, for Paul, is the culmination of the history of God's actions in Israel? How do each of the people he has mentioned point to this culmination? **7.** How did the rulers of Jerusalem fulfill the words of the prophets when they rejected Jesus? How do the Old Testament prophecies substantiate what happened? **8.** How does Paul's message compare with Peter's in chapter 2 and Stephen's in chapter 7? **9.** What kind of positive response does Paul's sermon generate (vv. 42-44)? What kind of negative response (v. 45)? Why? **10.** What is the relation between the influence of God's word and opposition to it? Is this an isolated example? What impact, positive and negative, does this rejection have on the church?

REFLECT: 1. When have you dropped out of a ministry? What happened? How do you feel about it now? **2.** What kind of opposition have you faced because of your faith? How do you usually respond to opposition? Does it derail you or make you stronger? Why? Would it be tougher for you to face opposition from community leaders or from family members? Why? **3.** What are the major events of your own personal history of God's dealings with you? How have each of these affected you? What do you see as the culmination of this history? How do the other events lead up to or look back on this event? How important is this history to your present walk with God? **4.** How would you characterize the relationship between the Old Testament and the New Testament? Do you think the New Testament could exist without the Old Testament? Why or why not? What place does the Old Testament have in your faith? In your witness of that faith?

ᵛ33 Or have begotten you   ʷ33 Psalm 2:7   ˣ34 Isaiah 55:3   ʸ35 Psalm 16:10   ᶻ41 Hab. 1:5

next Sabbath. [43]When the congregation was dismissed, many of the Jews and devout converts to Judaism followed Paul and Barnabas, who talked with them and urged them to continue in the grace of God.

[44]On the next Sabbath almost the whole city gathered to hear the word of the Lord. [45]When the Jews saw the crowds, they were filled with jealousy and talked abusively against what Paul was saying.

[46]Then Paul and Barnabas answered them boldly: "We had to speak the word of God to you first. Since you reject it and do not consider yourselves worthy of eternal life, we now turn to the Gentiles. [47]For this is what the Lord has commanded us:

" 'I have made you[a] a light for the Gentiles,
that you[a] may bring salvation to the ends of the earth.'[b]"

[48]When the Gentiles heard this, they were glad and honored the word of the Lord; and all who were appointed for eternal life believed.

[49]The word of the Lord spread through the whole region. [50]But the Jews incited the God-fearing women of high standing and the leading men of the city. They stirred up persecution against Paul and Barnabas, and expelled them from their region. [51]So they shook the dust from their feet in protest against them and went to Iconium. [52]And the disciples were filled with joy and with the Holy Spirit.

In Iconium

14 At Iconium Paul and Barnabas went as usual into the Jewish synagogue. There they spoke so effectively that a great number of Jews and Gentiles believed. [2]But the Jews who refused to believe stirred up the Gentiles and poisoned their minds against the brothers. [3]So Paul and Barnabas spent considerable time there, speaking boldly for the Lord, who confirmed the message of his grace by enabling them to do miraculous signs and wonders. [4]The people of the city were divided; some sided with the Jews, others with the apostles. [5]There was a plot afoot among the Gentiles and Jews, together with their leaders, to mistreat them and stone them. [6]But they found out about it and fled to the Lycaonian cities of Lystra and Derbe and to the surrounding country, [7]where they continued to preach the good news.

In Lystra and Derbe

[8]In Lystra there sat a man crippled in his feet, who was lame from birth and had never walked. [9]He listened to Paul as he was speaking. Paul looked directly at him, saw that he had faith to be healed [10]and called out, "Stand up on your feet!" At that, the man jumped up and began to walk.

[11]When the crowd saw what Paul had done, they shouted in the Lycaonian language, "The gods have come down to us in human form!" [12]Barnabas they called Zeus, and Paul they called

DIG: 1. Locate Iconium on a map. What is its relationship to Pisidian Antioch? 2. How does their experience in Iconium differ from their experience in Pisidian Antioch (13:13-52)? How is it similar? What characterizes their ministry here? What characterizes the opposition? What are the results of this persecution? How does the opposition affect the spread of the gospel?

REFLECT: How do you think you'd feel if you were constantly under siege like Paul and Barnabas? What advice would you have given them as they were run out of town? Why?

OPEN: With what mythological character do you most identify (Paul Bunyan, Zeus, Thor, Pecos Bill, etc.)? Why?

DIG: 1. Locate Lystra on a map. How far is Lystra from Iconium? From Antioch? 2. What is the result of the lame man's faith? What effect does this have on the crowd? Do you think this is the effect Paul hoped for? Why or why not? What does this tell you about human nature? How is this supported by verse 19? 3. How upset

[a]47 The Greek is singular.   [b]47 Isaiah 49:6

Hermes because he was the chief speaker. [13]The priest of Zeus, whose temple was just outside the city, brought bulls and wreaths to the city gates because he and the crowd wanted to offer sacrifices to them.

[14]But when the apostles Barnabas and Paul heard of this, they tore their clothes and rushed out into the crowd, shouting: [15]"Men, why are you doing this? We too are only men, human like you. We are bringing you good news, telling you to turn from these worthless things to the living God, who made heaven and earth and sea and everything in them. [16]In the past, he let all nations go their own way. [17]Yet he has not left himself without testimony: He has shown kindness by giving you rain from heaven and crops in their seasons; he provides you with plenty of food and fills your hearts with joy." [18]Even with these words, they had difficulty keeping the crowd from sacrificing to them.

[19]Then some Jews came from Antioch and Iconium and won the crowd over. They stoned Paul and dragged him outside the city, thinking he was dead. [20]But after the disciples had gathered around him, he got up and went back into the city. The next day he and Barnabas left for Derbe.

The Return to Antioch in Syria

[21]They preached the good news in that city and won a large number of disciples. Then they returned to Lystra, Iconium and Antioch, [22]strengthening the disciples and encouraging them to remain true to the faith. "We must go through many hardships to enter the kingdom of God," they said. [23]Paul and Barnabas appointed elders[c] for them in each church and, with prayer and fasting, committed them to the Lord, in whom they had put their trust. [24]After going through Pisidia, they came into Pamphylia, [25]and when they had preached the word in Perga, they went down to Attalia.

[26]From Attalia they sailed back to Antioch, where they had been committed to the grace of God for the work they had now completed. [27]On arriving there, they gathered the church together and reported all that God had done through them and how he had opened the door of faith to the Gentiles. [28]And they stayed there a long time with the disciples.

The Council at Jerusalem

15 Some men came down from Judea to Antioch and were teaching the brothers: "Unless you are circumcised, according to the custom taught by Moses, you cannot be saved." [2]This brought Paul and Barnabas into sharp dispute and debate with them. So Paul and Barnabas were appointed, along with some other believers, to go up to Jerusalem to see the apostles and elders about this question. [3]The church sent them on their way, and as they traveled through Phoenicia and Samaria, they told how the Gentiles had been converted. This news made all the brothers very glad. [4]When they came to Jerusalem, they were welcomed by the church and the apostles and elders, to

[c]23 Or *Barnabas ordained elders*; or *Barnabas had elders elected*

were the people from Antioch and Iconium? How does verse 19 support your answer? **4.** After reading verses 19-20, how would you characterize Paul? His supporters? How do you feel about John's desertion at Perga after reading these verses?

REFLECT: 1. When have you experienced rejection from people who were previously very positive about you? What happened? How well do you usually handle rejection? **2.** How willing are you to suffer persecution for your beliefs? What does this say about you? **3.** In what areas are you most easily swayed by other peoples' opinions? How does this affect your Christian faith? What can you do to remain strong in your faith? How will you begin strengthening your faith this week?

DIG: 1. Where is Derbe? How are the results of the ministry there different from anywhere else? **2.** Why do you think Paul and Barnabas return to the very cities in which they were opposed and persecuted? What does this say about the importance of follow-up ministry? **3.** How would you summarize this first missionary journey?

REFLECT: 1. How have you strengthened and encouraged other believers in the last two weeks? Who has been a great source of strength and encouragement to you during that time? **2.** How is your style of ministry and witnessing similar to that of Paul and Barnabas in this passage?

OPEN: When you were growing up, what religious rules were you required to follow? Why? How did you feel about this? How do you feel about it now?

DIG: 1. In general, how would you describe relations between Jews and Gentiles during this period of history? How long had the Jews been following God? How hard had they worked at remaining faithful to the one God? How does all this relate to the problem in this passage? **2.** Read Matthew 20:1-16. What parallels do you see between this parable and the dispute in this passage? **3.** Why would Paul and Barnabas be especially concerned with this problem? How would it affect their ministry if they had to circumcise all their converts? **4.** How does the background of those opposing Paul and Barnabas affect their view of the problem? Is this to be expected? Why or why not? **5.** What is Paul's background (see Acts 26:5)? What is Peter's position in the early church? Who is James (see Gal. 1:19)? What is James' importance in the Jerusalem church? What arguments do each of these men use to state their position? Why would these arguments and the backgrounds of each of these men be difficult to defeat? **6.** Do you think it is just coincidence that it is these three men arguing against the men in verse 5? What evidence do you see of God's special preparation for this problem in the church? **7.** How did the early church answer this question, On what terms can Gentiles be saved? Why do you think they included verse 20 in these terms?

REFLECT: 1. What do you think is essential to salvation? Why? **2.** In what ways do you or your church add on to the gospel in your relations with non-Christians or new believers? **3.** What baggage from your past have you had to unload to live a more productive life? What baggage have you found helpful? Why? **4.** If you were to make three suggestions to new believers about what might be helpful to their spiritual growth, what would you tell them? Why?

OPEN: What was the best news you received this week? Why was it so good?

DIG: 1. Why would a letter and representatives from the Jerusalem church be a good way to communicate the apostles' decision? **2.** How does the salutation communicate both authority and compassion? **3.** What is the tone of the letter? What would verse 24 communicate to the readers? Verses 25-27? Verses 28-29? **4.** How do Judas and Silas personally add to this letter? How are the unity and harmony of the church illustrated in verse 33? **5.** Why do you think Paul and

whom they reported everything God had done through them.

[5]Then some of the believers who belonged to the party of the Pharisees stood up and said, "The Gentiles must be circumcised and required to obey the law of Moses."

[6]The apostles and elders met to consider this question. [7]After much discussion, Peter got up and addressed them: "Brothers, you know that some time ago God made a choice among you that the Gentiles might hear from my lips the message of the gospel and believe. [8]God, who knows the heart, showed that he accepted them by giving the Holy Spirit to them, just as he did to us. [9]He made no distinction between us and them, for he purified their hearts by faith. [10]Now then, why do you try to test God by putting on the necks of the disciples a yoke that neither we nor our fathers have been able to bear? [11]No! We believe it is through the grace of our Lord Jesus that we are saved, just as they are."

[12]The whole assembly became silent as they listened to Barnabas and Paul telling about the miraculous signs and wonders God had done among the Gentiles through them. [13]When they finished, James spoke up: "Brothers, listen to me. [14]Simon[d] has described to us how God at first showed his concern by taking from the Gentiles a people for himself. [15]The words of the prophets are in agreement with this, as it is written:

[16]" 'After this I will return
    and rebuild David's fallen tent.
Its ruins I will rebuild,
    and I will restore it,
[17]that the remnant of men may seek the Lord,
    and all the Gentiles who bear my name,
    says the Lord, who does these things'[e]
[18]   that have been known for ages.[f]

[19]"It is my judgment, therefore, that we should not make it difficult for the Gentiles who are turning to God. [20]Instead we should write to them, telling them to abstain from food polluted by idols, from sexual immorality, from the meat of strangled animals and from blood. [21]For Moses has been preached in every city from the earliest times and is read in the synagogues on every Sabbath."

The Council's Letter to Gentile Believers

[22]Then the apostles and elders, with the whole church, decided to choose some of their own men and send them to Antioch with Paul and Barnabas. They chose Judas (called Barsabbas) and Silas, two men who were leaders among the brothers. [23]With them they sent the following letter:

The apostles and elders, your brothers,

To the Gentile believers in Antioch, Syria and Cilicia:

Greetings.

---

[d]14 Greek *Simeon*, a variant of *Simon;* that is, Peter   [e]17 Amos 9:11,12
[f]17,18 Some manuscripts *things'— / [18]known to the Lord for ages is his work*

[24]We have heard that some went out from us without our authorization and disturbed you, troubling your minds by what they said. [25]So we all agreed to choose some men and send them to you with our dear friends Barnabas and Paul— [26]men who have risked their lives for the name of our Lord Jesus Christ. [27]Therefore we are sending Judas and Silas to confirm by word of mouth what we are writing. [28]It seemed good to the Holy Spirit and to us not to burden you with anything beyond the following requirements: [29]You are to abstain from food sacrificed to idols, from blood, from the meat of strangled animals and from sexual immorality. You will do well to avoid these things.

Farewell.

[30]The men were sent off and went down to Antioch, where they gathered the church together and delivered the letter. [31]The people read it and were glad for its encouraging message. [32]Judas and Silas, who themselves were prophets, said much to encourage and strengthen the brothers. [33]After spending some time there, they were sent off by the brothers with the blessing of peace to return to those who had sent them.[g] [35]But Paul and Barnabas remained in Antioch, where they and many others taught and preached the word of the Lord.

Disagreement Between Paul and Barnabas

[36]Some time later Paul said to Barnabas, "Let us go back and visit the brothers in all the towns where we preached the word of the Lord and see how they are doing." [37]Barnabas wanted to take John, also called Mark, with them, [38]but Paul did not think it wise to take him, because he had deserted them in Pamphylia and had not continued with them in the work. [39]They had such a sharp disagreement that they parted company. Barnabas took Mark and sailed for Cyprus, [40]but Paul chose Silas and left, commended by the brothers to the grace of the Lord. [41]He went through Syria and Cilicia, strengthening the churches.

Timothy Joins Paul and Silas

16 He came to Derbe and then to Lystra, where a disciple named Timothy lived, whose mother was a Jewess and a believer, but whose father was a Greek. [2]The brothers at Lystra and Iconium spoke well of him. [3]Paul wanted to take him along on the journey, so he circumcised him because of the Jews who lived in that area, for they all knew that his father was a Greek. [4]As they traveled from town to town, they delivered the decisions reached by the apostles and elders in Jerusalem for the people to obey. [5]So the churches were strengthened in the faith and grew daily in numbers.

Barnabas remained in Antioch? What did they hope to accomplish here?

REFLECT: 1. From the debate, the resulting letter, and the way in which it was delivered, what do you learn about the way to solve disagreements among Christians? How is your style of handling disagreements similar to the way the issue was handled in chapter 15? Different from it? What would you like to change about the way you and your church handle disputes and disagreements? **2.** What else did you learn from this section about how to communicate? How were you encouraged this week? How important are positive, encouraging people in your life? What grade would you give yourself on how well you encouraged others this week? Why? Whom could you help that needs encouragement today? How?

DIG: 1. What are the negative results of this disagreement? The positive results? What do you learn about Paul and Barnabas in this passage? **2.** How does 2 Timothy 4:11 shed light on this story?

REFLECT: Who is now a teammate or friend of yours in spite of trouble in the past? What caused that relationship to improve? How can you agree to disagree yet still remain friends and teammates?

DIG: 1. To what kind of believers is Acts 15:1-29 addressed? How does this relate to Paul's circumcision of Timothy? Why do you think there is still this separation between Jew and Gentile in the church? **2.** How would this circumcision help Paul and Timothy in their ministry? **3.** Why do you think Paul returned to Lystra and Derbe? What does this teach you about working with new believers?

REFLECT: 1. How do you think your parents' heritage has affected your faith? Why? **2.** What have you learned from this passage about reaching people for Christ and then strengthening them in their new faith? How will you put this into practice this week?

---

[g]33 Some manuscripts *them,* [34]*but Silas decided to remain there*

DIG: How involved is God in directing this missionary journey? Why is this important?

REFLECT: 1. When has God closed a door in your life? What happened? How did you feel then? Now? **2.** Where do you see an open door now? What is it? What are your plans for this opportunity? **3.** How does God usually speak to you? How does he get your attention? How do you know it's God speaking and not someone else?

DIG: 1. Trace Paul and Silas' journey from Antioch on a map. Through which parts of the world have they gone? Which places has Paul revisited and which are new for him? **2.** What are God's part, Paul's part, and Lydia's part in her conversion? **3.** The gospel came to Europe through the conversion of Lydia. What does this say about the way God works?

REFLECT: If you had been in charge of bringing the gospel to Europe, what strategy do you think you'd have used? Why? How is God's strategy different from yours? What does this teach you?

OPEN: When was the last time you got a spanking? What do you remember about that? **2.** What song or hymn best describes your life, "I've Got Plenty of Nothing," "Battle Hymn of the Republic," etc.)? Why this song?

DIG: 1. Is the slave girl speaking the truth in verse 17? How does her speaking the truth become a hindrance to the truth? What does this tell you about the nature of the truth? **2.** In verse 13, why do you think Paul went down to the river to pray rather than to a synagogue? What does this say about the size of the Jewish population in this part of Macedonia? How does this relate to the charges against Paul and Silas in verses 20-21? How does it relate to the actions of the crowd and of the magistrates? **3.** Why do you suppose that Timothy and Luke are treated differently than Paul and Silas (v. 1)? How does this relate to the charges? **4.** Which do you find most surprising—Paul and Silas' actions in verse 25 or their actions in verse 28? Why? What do these actions tell you about Paul and Silas? Why do you think these actions have such a great

Paul's Vision of the Man of Macedonia

6Paul and his companions traveled throughout the region of Phrygia and Galatia, having been kept by the Holy Spirit from preaching the word in the province of Asia. 7When they came to the border of Mysia, they tried to enter Bithynia, but the Spirit of Jesus would not allow them to. 8So they passed by Mysia and went down to Troas. 9During the night Paul had a vision of a man of Macedonia standing and begging him, "Come over to Macedonia and help us." 10After Paul had seen the vision, we got ready at once to leave for Macedonia, concluding that God had called us to preach the gospel to them.

Lydia's Conversion in Philippi

11From Troas we put out to sea and sailed straight for Samothrace, and the next day on to Neapolis. 12From there we traveled to Philippi, a Roman colony and the leading city of that district of Macedonia. And we stayed there several days.

13On the Sabbath we went outside the city gate to the river, where we expected to find a place of prayer. We sat down and began to speak to the women who had gathered there. 14One of those listening was a woman named Lydia, a dealer in purple cloth from the city of Thyatira, who was a worshiper of God. The Lord opened her heart to respond to Paul's message. 15When she and the members of her household were baptized, she invited us to her home. "If you consider me a believer in the Lord," she said, "come and stay at my house." And she persuaded us.

Paul and Silas in Prison

16Once when we were going to the place of prayer, we were met by a slave girl who had a spirit by which she predicted the future. She earned a great deal of money for her owners by fortune-telling. 17This girl followed Paul and the rest of us, shouting, "These men are servants of the Most High God, who are telling you the way to be saved." 18She kept this up for many days. Finally Paul became so troubled that he turned around and said to the spirit, "In the name of Jesus Christ I command you to come out of her!" At that moment the spirit left her.

19When the owners of the slave girl realized that their hope of making money was gone, they seized Paul and Silas and dragged them into the marketplace to face the authorities. 20They brought them before the magistrates and said, "These men are Jews, and are throwing our city into an uproar 21by advocating customs unlawful for us Romans to accept or practice."

22The crowd joined in the attack against Paul and Silas, and the magistrates ordered them to be stripped and beaten. 23After they had been severely flogged, they were thrown into prison, and the jailer was commanded to guard them carefully. 24Upon receiving such orders, he put them in the inner cell and fastened their feet in the stocks.

25About midnight Paul and Silas were praying and singing hymns to God, and the other prisoners were listening to them. 26Suddenly there was such a violent earthquake that the foundations of the prison were shaken. At once all the prison doors flew open, and everybody's chains came loose. [27]The jailer woke up, and when he saw the prison doors open, he drew his sword and was about to kill himself because he thought the prisoners had escaped. [28]But Paul shouted, "Don't harm yourself! We are all here!"

[29]The jailer called for lights, rushed in and fell trembling before Paul and Silas. [30]He then brought them out and asked, "Sirs, what must I do to be saved?"

[31]They replied, "Believe in the Lord Jesus, and you will be saved—you and your household." [32]Then they spoke the word of the Lord to him and to all the others in his house. [33]At that hour of the night the jailer took them and washed their wounds; then immediately he and all his family were baptized. [34]The jailer brought them into his house and set a meal before them; he was filled with joy because he had come to believe in God—he and his whole family.

[35]When it was daylight, the magistrates sent their officers to the jailer with the order: "Release those men." [36]The jailer told Paul, "The magistrates have ordered that you and Silas be released. Now you can leave. Go in peace."

[37]But Paul said to the officers: "They beat us publicly without a trial, even though we are Roman citizens, and threw us into prison. And now do they want to get rid of us quietly? No! Let them come themselves and escort us out."

[38]The officers reported this to the magistrates, and when they heard that Paul and Silas were Roman citizens, they were alarmed. [39]They came to appease them and escorted them from the prison, requesting them to leave the city. [40]After Paul and Silas came out of the prison, they went to Lydia's house, where they met with the brothers and encouraged them. Then they left.

In Thessalonica

17 When they had passed through Amphipolis and Apollonia, they came to Thessalonica, where there was a Jewish synagogue. [2]As his custom was, Paul went into the synagogue, and on three Sabbath days he reasoned with them from the Scriptures, [3]explaining and proving that the Christ[h] had to suffer and rise from the dead. "This Jesus I am proclaiming to you is the Christ,[h]" he said. [4]Some of the Jews were persuaded and joined Paul and Silas, as did a large number of God-fearing Greeks and not a few prominent women.

[5]But the Jews were jealous; so they rounded up some bad characters from the marketplace, formed a mob and started a riot in the city. They rushed to Jason's house in search of Paul and Silas in order to bring them out to the crowd.[i] [6]But when they did not find them, they dragged Jason and some other brothers before the city officials, shouting: "These men who have caused trouble all over the world have now come here, [7]and Jason has welcomed them into his house. They are all defying Caesar's decrees, saying that there is another king, one called

[h]3 Or Messiah   [i]5 Or the assembly of the people

OPEN: Who have been the four most important women in your life? Why?

DIG: 1. What new cities are mentioned here? Where are they located? 2. How would you describe Paul's strategy in Thessalonica? How is this similar to his strategy in other places? 3. What are the results of this strategy? How is this similar to the results in other cities Paul has visited? 4. Do you think Paul could prevent the riots by changing his strategy? Why or why not? How might a change affect the other results of Paul's preaching? What do you learn about Paul from this?

REFLECT: 1. How would you describe your ministry strategy? How would you describe your effectiveness in ministry? How is this related to your strategy? 2. How could you change your strategy to become more effective? What will you do today to begin this change?

effect on the jailer? What does this say about the power of God to work in difficult situations? 5. What do you think Paul hopes to accomplish by his demand in verse 37? Who would Paul be most concerned with in this town (v. 40)? How would Paul's demand be of help to these people?

REFLECT: 1. Whom have you unintentionally offended because of your faith? What were your feelings? 2. How does music affect you when you are troubled? What songs are most comforting to you? 3. If a person asked you, "What must I do to be saved?", how would you answer? 4. How well do you think you would perform in circumstances similar to Paul and Silas'? Why do you think Paul and Silas were able to perform as well as they did? What can you learn from this? How will you apply what you have learned to your life today?

Jesus." [8]When they heard this, the crowd and the city officials were thrown into turmoil. [9]Then they made Jason and the others post bond and let them go.

In Berea

[10]As soon as it was night, the brothers sent Paul and Silas away to Berea. On arriving there, they went to the Jewish synagogue. [11]Now the Bereans were of more noble character than the Thessalonians, for they received the message with great eagerness and examined the Scriptures every day to see if what Paul said was true. [12]Many of the Jews believed, as did also a number of prominent Greek women and many Greek men.

[13]When the Jews in Thessalonica learned that Paul was preaching the word of God at Berea, they went there too, agitating the crowds and stirring them up. [14]The brothers immediately sent Paul to the coast, but Silas and Timothy stayed at Berea. [15]The men who escorted Paul brought him to Athens and then left with instructions for Silas and Timothy to join him as soon as possible.

In Athens

[16]While Paul was waiting for them in Athens, he was greatly distressed to see that the city was full of idols. [17]So he reasoned in the synagogue with the Jews and the God-fearing Greeks, as well as in the marketplace day by day with those who happened to be there. [18]A group of Epicurean and Stoic philosophers began to dispute with him. Some of them asked, "What is this babbler trying to say?" Others remarked, "He seems to be advocating foreign gods." They said this because Paul was preaching the good news about Jesus and the resurrection. [19]Then they took him and brought him to a meeting of the Areopagus, where they said to him, "May we know what this new teaching is that you are presenting? [20]You are bringing some strange ideas to our ears, and we want to know what they mean." [21](All the Athenians and the foreigners who lived there spent their time doing nothing but talking about and listening to the latest ideas.)

[22]Paul then stood up in the meeting of the Areopagus and said: "Men of Athens! I see that in every way you are very religious. [23]For as I walked around and looked carefully at your objects of worship, I even found an altar with this inscription: TO AN UNKNOWN GOD. Now what you worship as something unknown I am going to proclaim to you.

[24]"The God who made the world and everything in it is the Lord of heaven and earth and does not live in temples built by hands. [25]And he is not served by human hands, as if he needed anything, because he himself gives all men life and breath and everything else. [26]From one man he made every nation of men, that they should inhabit the whole earth; and he determined the times set for them and the exact places where they should live. [27]God did this so that men would seek him and perhaps reach out for him and find him, though he is not far from each one of us. [28]'For in him we live and move and have our being.' As some of your own poets have said, 'We are his offspring.'

29"Therefore since we are God's offspring, we should not think that the divine being is like gold or silver or stone—an image made by man's design and skill. 30In the past God overlooked such ignorance, but now he commands all people everywhere to repent. 31For he has set a day when he will judge the world with justice by the man he has appointed. He has given proof of this to all men by raising him from the dead."

32When they heard about the resurrection of the dead, some of them sneered, but others said, "We want to hear you again on this subject." 33At that, Paul left the Council. 34A few men became followers of Paul and believed. Among them was Dionysius, a member of the Areopagus, also a woman named Damaris, and a number of others.

In Corinth

18 After this, Paul left Athens and went to Corinth. 2There he met a Jew named Aquila a native of Pontus, who had recently come from Italy with his wife Priscilla, because Claudius had ordered all the Jews to leave Rome. Paul went to see them, 3and because he was a tentmaker as they were, he stayed and worked with them. 4Every Sabbath he reasoned in the synagogue, trying to persuade Jews and Greeks.

5When Silas and Timothy came from Macedonia, Paul devoted himself exclusively to preaching, testifying to the Jews that Jesus was the Christ.*ʲ* 6But when the Jews opposed Paul and became abusive, he shook out his clothes in protest and said to them, "Your blood be on your own heads! I am clear of my responsibility. From now on I will go to the Gentiles."

7Then Paul left the synagogue and went next door to the house of Titius Justus, a worshiper of God. 8Crispus, the synagogue ruler, and his entire household believed in the Lord; and many of the Corinthians who heard him believed and were baptized.

9One night the Lord spoke to Paul in a vision: "Do not be afraid; keep on speaking, do not be silent. 10For I am with you, and no one is going to attack and harm you, because I have many people in this city." 11So Paul stayed for a year and a half, teaching them the word of God.

12While Gallio was proconsul of Achaia, the Jews made a united attack on Paul and brought him into court. 13"This man," they charged, "is persuading the people to worship God in ways contrary to the law."

14Just as Paul was about to speak, Gallio said to the Jews, "If you Jews were making a complaint about some misdemeanor or serious crime, it would be reasonable for me to listen to you. 15But since it involves questions about words and names and your own law—settle the matter yourselves. I will not be a judge of such things." 16So he had them ejected from the court. 17Then they all turned on Sosthenes the synagogue ruler and beat him in front of the court. But Gallio showed no concern whatever.

REFLECT: 1. What distresses you spiritually about the city in which you live? What specific needs do you see? What do you feel God is calling you to do about your city? **2.** Paul tried to reach out to those who had very little background and touch them with the gospel. What do you learn from him about how to share your faith? **3.** How true is this statement for you, "In him we live and move and have our being"? Why?

OPEN: Who was your first friend when you moved to the place where you live now? What caused you to become good friends?

DIG: 1. What do you know about the city of Corinth (see Introduction to 1 Corinthians)? **2.** What are the three stages in Paul's ministry in Corinth (vv. 4, 7, 14)? What problem does he face at each stage? What opportunities? **3.** Why does Paul preach the gospel to the Jews first? What does this imply about God's view of the Jews? **4.** What does verse 5 say about Silas and Timothy's role in Paul's ministry? How important is this role? Why? **5.** Why would the vision in verse 9 be a comfort to Paul? Why would Paul need this extra comfort? What is the result of this vision? **6.** Why would the Jews turn on Sosthenes rather than Paul in verse 17? What does this say about the validity of their charges against Paul? About God's protection of Paul?

REFLECT: 1. How important is Christian fellowship in a pagan culture? How would you characterize the quality of the Christian fellowship you experience? How could it be better? **2.** If the Lord spoke to you in a vision tonight about your circumstances and what he had in mind for you, what would he probably say? Why? **3.** In looking back over your life, what stages have you gone through? What problems did you face at each stage? What opportunities? What part did God play in each stage of your life?

ʲ5 Or *Messiah;* also in verse 28

OPEN: As a child, whose absence affected you the most? Why?

DIG: 1. Where does Paul go after Corinth? What do you know about this place (see a Bible dictionary or encyclopedia)? 2. If the first missionary trip centered on evangelism and numerical growth (14:21-25), what does this second journey focus on (vv. 23; 16:5)? What do you learn from this? 3. How would Apollo's skill in debate help the believers of Achaia? How does his ministry in Achaia complement Paul's in Galatia and Phrygia? How important does his ministry seem to be? Why?

REFLECT: 1. When have you taken a vow for spiritual reasons? What happened? What did you learn? 2. Who was very helpful to you when you were young and enthusiastic about the faith? How did this person help? 3. How does your church balance evangelism with the strengthening and equipping of believers?

Priscilla, Aquila and Apollos

[18]Paul stayed on in Corinth for some time. Then he left the brothers and sailed for Syria, accompanied by Priscilla and Aquila. Before he sailed, he had his hair cut off at Cenchrea because of a vow he had taken. [19]They arrived at Ephesus, where Paul left Priscilla and Aquila. He himself went into the synagogue and reasoned with the Jews. [20]When they asked him to spend more time with them, he declined. [21]But as he left, he promised, "I will come back if it is God's will." Then he set sail from Ephesus. [22]When he landed at Caesarea, he went up and greeted the church and then went down to Antioch.

[23]After spending some time in Antioch, Paul set out from there and traveled from place to place throughout the region of Galatia and Phrygia, strengthening all the disciples.

[24]Meanwhile a Jew named Apollos, a native of Alexandria, came to Ephesus. He was a learned man, with a thorough knowledge of the Scriptures. [25]He had been instructed in the way of the Lord, and he spoke with great fervor[k] and taught about Jesus accurately, though he knew only the baptism of John. [26]He began to speak boldly in the synagogue. When Priscilla and Aquila heard him, they invited him to their home and explained to him the way of God more adequately.

[27]When Apollos wanted to go to Achaia, the brothers encouraged him and wrote to the disciples there to welcome him. On arriving, he was a great help to those who by grace had believed. [28]For he vigorously refuted the Jews in public debate, proving from the Scriptures that Jesus was the Christ.

Paul in Ephesus

19 While Apollos was at Corinth, Paul took the road through the interior and arrived at Ephesus. There he found some disciples [2]and asked them, "Did you receive the Holy Spirit when[l] you believed?"

They answered, "No, we have not even heard that there is a Holy Spirit."

[3]So Paul asked, "Then what baptism did you receive?"

"John's baptism," they replied.

[4]Paul said, "John's baptism was a baptism of repentance. He told the people to believe in the one coming after him, that is, in Jesus." [5]On hearing this, they were baptized into[m] the name of the Lord Jesus. [6]When Paul placed his hands on them, the Holy Spirit came on them, and they spoke in tongues[n] and prophesied. [7]There were about twelve men in all.

[8]Paul entered the synagogue and spoke boldly there for three months, arguing persuasively about the kingdom of God. [9]But some of them became obstinate; they refused to believe and publicly maligned the Way. So Paul left them. He took the disciples with him and had discussions daily in the lecture hall of Tyrannus. [10]This went on for two years, so that all the Jews and Greeks who lived in the province of Asia heard the word of the Lord.

OPEN: What do you believe about evil spirits, ouija boards, witches, ghosts?

DIG: 1. How is John's baptism different than being baptized in Jesus' name? Why isn't John's baptism enough? 2. Why is it important that these believers receive the Holy Spirit? How would this help their belief? How would it affect their view of John's baptism? 3. What seems to be the signal throughout Acts for Paul to stop teaching in the synagogue? Why do you think this is so? What does it teach you about ministry in general? 4. Make a list of the major events of Paul's life to this point in the Book of Acts. In evaluating Paul's life since the first mention of him in 8:1, how do you find he has changed? How gradually has this change taken place? What are the major factors in this transformation? 5. Why do you think nonbelievers would use Jesus' name to cast out demons? Why do you think the demons would not respond to these men? What does this say about the power of Jesus' name? 6. Why would the events of verses 13-16 cause the events of verses 18-19?

[k]25 Or *with fervor in the Spirit*   [l]2 Or *after*   [m]5 Or *in*   [n]6 Or *other languages*

[11]God did extraordinary miracles through Paul, [12]so that even handkerchiefs and aprons that had touched him were taken to the sick, and their illnesses were cured and the evil spirits left them.

[13]Some Jews who went around driving out evil spirits tried to invoke the name of the Lord Jesus over those who were demon-possessed. They would say, "In the name of Jesus, whom Paul preaches, I command you to come out." [14]Seven sons of Sceva, a Jewish chief priest, were doing this. [15]One day, the evil spirit answered them, "Jesus I know, and I know about Paul, but who are you?" [16]Then the man who had the evil spirit jumped on them and overpowered them all. He gave them such a beating that they ran out of the house naked and bleeding.

[17]When this became known to the Jews and Greeks living in Ephesus, they were all seized with fear, and the name of the Lord Jesus was held in high honor. [18]Many of those who believed now came and openly confessed their evil deeds. [19]A number who had practiced sorcery brought their scrolls together and burned them publicly. When they calculated the value of the scrolls, the total came to fifty thousand drachmas. [o] [20]In this way the word of the Lord spread widely and grew in power.

[21]After all this had happened, Paul decided to go to Jerusalem, passing through Macedonia and Achaia. "After I have been there," he said, "I must visit Rome also." [22]He sent two of his helpers, Timothy and Erastus, to Macedonia, while he stayed in the province of Asia a little longer.

The Riot in Ephesus

[23]About that time there arose a great disturbance about the Way. [24]A silversmith named Demetrius, who made silver shrines of Artemis, brought in no little business for the craftsmen. [25]He called them together, along with the workmen in related trades, and said: "Men, you know we receive a good income from this business. [26]And you see and hear how this fellow Paul has convinced and led astray large numbers of people here in Ephesus and in practically the whole province of Asia. He says that man-made gods are no gods at all. [27]There is danger not only that our trade will lose its good name, but also that the temple of the great goddess Artemis will be discredited, and the goddess herself, who is worshiped throughout the province of Asia and the world, will be robbed of her divine majesty."

[28]When they heard this, they were furious and began shouting: "Great is Artemis of the Ephesians!" [29]Soon the whole city was in an uproar. The people seized Gaius Aristarchus, Paul's traveling companions from Macedonia, and rushed as one man into the theater. [30]Paul wanted to appear before the crowd, but the disciples would not let him. [31]Even some of the officials of the province, friends of Paul, sent him a message begging him not to venture into the theater.

[32]The assembly was in confusion: Some were shouting one thing, some another. Most of the people did not even know why

[o]19 A drachma was a silver coin worth about a day's wages.

What does this tell you about the seriousness of faith in Christ? **7.** How would you summarize this second missionary journey? How does your summary compare with the summary in verse 20?

REFLECT: 1. When have you been hampered by inadequate teaching in the faith? Who finally helped you more fully understand the truth? Have you ever been guilty of teaching inadequate truth? How seriously do you take the role of teacher (see James 3:1)? **2.** When have you had to walk away from a situation rather than stay? What did you learn? **3.** What spiritual counterfeits have you noticed in modern culture? How do you distinguish the real from the counterfeit? What resources have you found helpful in understanding spiritual counterfeits? **4.** What has characterized repentance in your life? What did it cost you to become a believer?

OPEN: Have you ever been caught in a riot or mob scene? What happened? What do you think causes such behavior?

DIG: 1. What two reasons does Demetrius give for wanting to get rid of the Way? Which of these seems to be most important to Demetrius and his fellow craftsmen? How do they use the other reason to legitimize their complaint? Why would this second reason be more likely to arouse the people than their true concern? **2.** What do you learn about the crowd from verse 32? Why would this situation be particularly dangerous for Paul? Are the craftsmen successful at this point in their plans? **3.** What is the main concern of the city clerk? How does this concern clash with the concern of the craftsmen? What is the ultimate cause of the failure of the craftsmen's plan?

REFLECT: 1. How has your relationship to Jesus Christ affected your business and wealth? Why? **2.** From what do you need to protect your spiritual leaders today? How? Why? From what do you need protection? **3.** Are religious feelings used today to sway public opinion? What examples can you think of? What are the dangers of such manipulation? What does this passage teach you about these dangers? What can Christians do to avoid these dangers?

DIG: 1. From verse 2, how would you characterize Paul's ministry in three words or less? 2. What does the increasing number of new names among Paul's traveling companions say about his ministry?

REFLECT: 1. If you could do a short-term mission project anywhere in the world, where would you want to go? Why? 2. What is your experience with mission projects? What was the first one you ever went on? Who invited you? 3. Which do you prefer—being part of a ministry team or working alone? Why? Which is more effective?

OPEN: What's one of the funniest things you've ever seen happen in church?

DIG: Based on this account, how would you describe Paul? What seems to be his main concern? How urgent is this concern for him? How do Paul's actions show his concerns?

REFLECT: 1. How spiritually alert are you now? Why? What could you do to become more alert? 2. What is the truth for you in this story? How could you apply it this week?

they were there. [33]The Jews pushed Alexander to the front, and some of the crowd shouted instructions to him. He motioned for silence in order to make a defense before the people. [34]But when they realized he was a Jew, they all shouted in unison for about two hours: "Great is Artemis of the Ephesians!"

[35]The city clerk quieted the crowd and said: "Men of Ephesus, doesn't all the world know that the city of Ephesus is the guardian of the temple of the great Artemis and of her image, which fell from heaven? [36]Therefore, since these facts are undeniable, you ought to be quiet and not do anything rash. [37]You have brought these men here, though they have neither robbed temples nor blasphemed our goddess. [38]If, then, Demetrius and his fellow craftsmen have a grievance against anybody, the courts are open and there are proconsuls. They can press charges. [39]If there is anything further you want to bring up, it must be settled in a legal assembly. [40]As it is, we are in danger of being charged with rioting because of today's events. In that case we would not be able to account for this commotion, since there is no reason for it." [41]After he had said this, he dismissed the assembly.

Through Macedonia and Greece

20 When the uproar had ended, Paul sent for the disciples and, after encouraging them, said good-by and set out for Macedonia. [2]He traveled through that area, speaking many words of encouragement to the people, and finally arrived in Greece, [3]where he stayed three months. Because the Jews made a plot against him just as he was about to sail for Syria, he decided to go back through Macedonia. [4]He was accompanied by Sopater son of Pyrrhus from Berea, Aristarchus and Secundus from Thessalonica, Gaius from Derbe, Timothy also, Tychicus and Trophimus from the province of Asia. [5]These men went on ahead and waited for us at Troas. [6]But we sailed from Philippi after the Feast of Unleavened Bread, and five days later joined the others at Troas, where we stayed seven days.

Eutychus Raised From the Dead at Troas

[7]On the first day of the week we came together to break bread. Paul spoke to the people and, because he intended to leave the next day, kept on talking until midnight. [8]There were many lamps in the upstairs room where we were meeting. [9]Seated in a window was a young man named Eutychus, who was sinking into a deep sleep as Paul talked on and on. When he was sound asleep, he fell to the ground from the third story and was picked up dead. [10]Paul went down, threw himself on the young man and put his arms around him. "Don't be alarmed," he said. "He's alive!" [11]Then he went upstairs again and broke bread and ate. After talking until daylight, he left. [12]The people took the young man home alive and were greatly comforted.

Paul's Farewell to the Ephesian Elders

[13]We went on ahead to the ship and sailed for Assos, where we were going to take Paul aboard. He had made this arrangement because he was going there on foot. [14]When he met us at Assos, we took him aboard and went on to Mitylene. [15]The next day we set sail from there and arrived off Kios. The day after that we crossed over to Samos, and on the following day arrived at Miletus. [16]Paul had decided to sail past Ephesus to avoid spending time in the province of Asia, for he was in a hurry to reach Jerusalem, if possible, by the day of Pentecost.

[17]From Miletus, Paul sent to Ephesus for the elders of the church. [18]When they arrived, he said to them: "You know how I lived the whole time I was with you, from the first day I came into the province of Asia. [19]I served the Lord with great humility and with tears, although I was severely tested by the plots of the Jews. [20]You know that I have not hesitated to preach anything that would be helpful to you but have taught you publicly and from house to house. [21]I have declared to both Jews and Greeks that they must turn to God in repentance and have faith in our Lord Jesus.

[22]"And now, compelled by the Spirit, I am going to Jerusalem, not knowing what will happen to me there. [23]I only know that in every city the Holy Spirit warns me that prison and hardships are facing me. [24]However, I consider my life worth nothing to me, if only I may finish the race and complete the task the Lord Jesus has given me—the task of testifying to the gospel of God's grace.

[25]"Now I know that none of you among whom I have gone about preaching the kingdom will ever see me again. [26]Therefore, I declare to you today that I am innocent of the blood of all men. [27]For I have not hesitated to proclaim to you the whole will of God. [28]Keep watch over yourselves and all the flock of which the Holy Spirit has made you overseers.[p] Be shepherds of the church of God,[q] which he bought with his own blood. [29]I know that after I leave, savage wolves will come in among you and will not spare the flock. [30]Even from your own number men will arise and distort the truth in order to draw away disciples after them. [31]So be on your guard! Remember that for three years I never stopped warning each of you night and day with tears.

[32]"Now I commit you to God and to the word of his grace, which can build you up and give you an inheritance among all those who are sanctified. [33]I have not coveted anyone's silver or gold or clothing. [34]You yourselves know that these hands of mine have supplied my own needs and the needs of my companions. [35]In everything I did, I showed you that by this kind of hard work we must help the weak, remembering the words the Lord Jesus himself said: 'It is more blessed to give than to receive.' "

[36]When he had said this, he knelt down with all of them and

OPEN: What has been one of the saddest farewells of your life? What happened?

DIG: 1. What arrangements has Paul made for this journey? What is the itinerary (trace it on a map)? 2. What is the significance of the day of Pentecost for the early church? For the Jews? Why would Pentecost cause Paul to hurry to such an extent? 3. What word would you use to characterize the tone of Paul's words in verses 18-31? Why this word? What seems to be the theme of these verses? How does your word support this theme? 4. How does the tone of Paul's message change in verses 32-35? What is Paul's concern in these verses? How does this relate to his concern in verses 18-31? 5. In summary, what does Paul say about his behavior, his service, his preaching, and his overriding ambition? 6. In chapter 20, what part do personal example, fellowship, and instruction play in the strengthening and encouraging of young churches?

REFLECT: 1. How hurried is your life? Would you characterize it as legitimate or senseless hurry? Why? 2. When have you served in a position of leadership in your church? How was your preparation similar to and different from the preparation Paul gave these elders? How would you like to see leadership training modified in your church? 3. What is your spiritual race? How well are you competing in it? 4. What are some warnings you wish people had given you? If you could give two warnings to a group of new Christians, what would you say? Why? 5. How does God's word strengthen you? 6. How have you experienced the truth of "it is more blessed to give than to receive" this year?

[p]28 Traditionally bishops   [q]28 Many manuscripts of the Lord

prayed. ³⁷They all wept as they embraced him and kissed him. ³⁸What grieved them most was his statement that they would never see his face again. Then they accompanied him to the ship.

On to Jerusalem

21 After we had torn ourselves away from them, we put out to sea and sailed straight to Cos. The next day we went to Rhodes and from there to Patara. ²We found a ship crossing over to Phoenicia, went on board and set sail. ³After sighting Cyprus and passing to the south of it, we sailed on to Syria. We landed at Tyre, where our ship was to unload its cargo. ⁴Finding the disciples there, we stayed with them seven days. Through the Spirit they urged Paul not to go on to Jerusalem. ⁵But when our time was up, we left and continued on our way. All the disciples and their wives and children accompanied us out of the city, and there on the beach we knelt to pray. ⁶After saying good-by to each other, we went aboard the ship, and they returned home.

⁷We continued our voyage from Tyre and landed at Ptolemais, where we greeted the brothers and stayed with them for a day. ⁸Leaving the next day, we reached Caesarea and stayed at the house of Philip the evangelist, one of the Seven. ⁹He had four unmarried daughters who prophesied.

¹⁰After we had been there a number of days, a prophet named Agabus came down from Judea. ¹¹Coming over to us, he took Paul's belt, tied his own hands and feet with it and said, "The Holy Spirit says, 'In this way the Jews of Jerusalem will bind the owner of this belt and will hand him over to the Gentiles.' "

¹²When we heard this, we and the people there pleaded with Paul not to go up to Jerusalem. ¹³Then Paul answered, "Why are you weeping and breaking my heart? I am ready not only to be bound, but also to die in Jerusalem for the name of the Lord Jesus." ¹⁴When he would not be dissuaded, we gave up and said, "The Lord's will be done."

¹⁵After this, we got ready and went up to Jerusalem. ¹⁶Some of the disciples from Caesarea accompanied us and brought us to the home of Mnason, where we were to stay. He was a man from Cyprus and one of the early disciples.

Paul's Arrival at Jerusalem

¹⁷When we arrived at Jerusalem, the brothers received us warmly. ¹⁸The next day Paul and the rest of us went to see James, and all the elders were present. ¹⁹Paul greeted them and reported in detail what God had done among the Gentiles through his ministry.

²⁰When they heard this, they praised God. Then they said to Paul: "You see, brother, how many thousands of Jews have believed, and all of them are zealous for the law. ²¹They have been informed that you teach all the Jews who live among the Gentiles to turn away from Moses, telling them not to circumcise their children or live according to our customs. ²²What shall we do? They will certainly hear that you have come, ²³so do what we tell you. There are four men with us who have made a vow. ²⁴Take these men, join in their purification rites and pay their

expenses, so that they can have their heads shaved. Then everybody will know there is no truth in these reports about you, but that you yourself are living in obedience to the law. ²⁵As for the Gentile believers, we have written to them our decision that they should abstain from food sacrificed to idols, from blood, from the meat of strangled animals and from sexual immorality."

²⁶The next day Paul took the men and purified himself along with them. Then he went to the temple to give notice of the date when the days of purification would end and the offering would be made for each of them.

Paul Arrested

²⁷When the seven days were nearly over, some Jews from the province of Asia saw Paul at the temple. They stirred up the whole crowd and seized him, ²⁸shouting, "Men of Israel, help us! This is the man who teaches all men everywhere against our people and our law and this place. And besides, he has brought Greeks into the temple area and defiled this holy place." ²⁹(They had previously seen Trophimus the Ephesian in the city with Paul and assumed that Paul had brought him into the temple area.)

³⁰The whole city was aroused, and the people came running from all directions. Seizing Paul, they dragged him from the temple, and immediately the gates were shut. ³¹While they were trying to kill him, news reached the commander of the Roman troops that the whole city of Jerusalem was in an uproar. ³²He at once took some officers and soldiers and ran down to the crowd. When the rioters saw the commander and his soldiers, they stopped beating Paul.

³³The commander came up and arrested him and ordered him to be bound with two chains. Then he asked who he was and what he had done. ³⁴Some in the crowd shouted one thing and some another, and since the commander could not get at the truth because of the uproar, he ordered that Paul be taken into the barracks. ³⁵When Paul reached the steps, the violence of the mob was so great he had to be carried by the soldiers. ³⁶The crowd that followed kept shouting, "Away with him!"

Paul Speaks to the Crowd

³⁷As the soldiers were about to take Paul into the barracks, he asked the commander, "May I say something to you?"

"Do you speak Greek?" he replied. ³⁸"Aren't you the Egyptian who started a revolt and led four thousand terrorists out into the desert some time ago?"

³⁹Paul answered, "I am a Jew, from Tarsus in Cilicia, a citizen of no ordinary city. Please let me speak to the people."

⁴⁰Having received the commander's permission, Paul stood on the steps and motioned to the crowd. When they were all **22** silent, he said to them in Aramaic ʳ: ¹"Brothers and fathers, listen now to my defense."

²When they heard him speak to them in Aramaic, they became very quiet.

ʳ40 Or possibly *Hebrew;* also in 22:2

REFLECT: 1. What principles determined Paul's actions here (see Acts 20:24; 1 Cor. 9:20-23; 10:32-33)? In what situation you currently face are some of these principles needed? How? 2. In what areas of your life do you need more purity? How could you experience a purification rite in those areas?

OPEN: When was the first time you ever had an encounter with a police officer? What happened?

DIG: 1. What seems to be the source of conflict between Paul and the people who seize him? What are the charges that they make against him? How are these charges similar to the charges that Jewish Christians have been making against him in the previous passage? 2. How is the situation similar to the one Jesus endured (there are at least five parallels) and the one Stephen experienced in Jerusalem? What does this say about the relationship between Jews and Christians in Jerusalem?

REFLECT: 1. When have incorrect stories been told about you? What happened? How did you deal with untruth? What did God teach you in that situation? 2. What one group do you think is most critical of the church today? What could be done to lessen the misunderstanding between the two? What can you do to help this process?

OPEN: When was the first time you gave your personal testimony? Why did you give it? What were the results? How did you feel as you were giving it? How do you feel about it now?

DIG: 1. Why do you think Paul wanted to address the crowd that had been beating him only moments before? How does this relate to Paul's statement in Acts 21:13? What does this say about Paul's character? 2. Why would the language Paul speaks quiet the crowd so quickly? How many references are there to matters of Paul's Jewish heritage? What do you think Paul is trying to do by speaking to this crowd in a very Jewish manner? How is this related to the charges made against Paul? **3.** Do you think Paul has compromised his beliefs by emphasizing his Jewishness? Why or why not? **4.** What is the heart of Paul's message in this speech? Do you think he was successful? Why or why not?

REFLECT: 1. Paul used a personal testimony in addressing this group. What would have happened if he'd preached a sermon? Why are personal testimonies effective? When do you find your story most effective and helpful to others? **2.** What else do you learn about communication techniques from Paul? How could you apply some of these skills in the weeks ahead? **3.** Paul is uniquely qualified to take the message to the Jews, but God calls him to the Gentiles. What do you learn from that? How is that truth helpful to you? **4.** What impresses you most about Paul here? How can you use this in your own life?

OPEN: How did your brothers and sisters deliberately antagonize you when you were growing up? How successful were they? How would you usually get even?

DIG: 1. Why does the crowd ultimately turn against Paul? What does this have to do with the charges against Paul (v. 28)? Why would Paul's statement have made them so angry? **2.** Of what importance is it that Paul was a Roman citizen? How did this help spread the gospel?

Then Paul said: [3]"I am a Jew, born in Tarsus of Cilicia, but brought up in this city. Under Gamaliel I was thoroughly trained in the law of our fathers and was just as zealous for God as any of you are today. [4]I persecuted the followers of this Way to their death, arresting both men and women and throwing them into prison, [5]as also the high priest and all the Council can testify. I even obtained letters from them to their brothers in Damascus, and went there to bring these people as prisoners to Jerusalem to be punished.

[6]"About noon as I came near Damascus, suddenly a bright light from heaven flashed around me. [7]I fell to the ground and heard a voice say to me, 'Saul! Saul! Why do you persecute me?'

[8]" 'Who are you, Lord?' I asked.

" 'I am Jesus of Nazareth, whom you are persecuting,' he replied. [9]My companions saw the light, but they did not understand the voice of him who was speaking to me.

[10]" 'What shall I do, Lord?' I asked.

" 'Get up,' the Lord said, 'and go into Damascus. There you will be told all that you have been assigned to do.' [11]My companions led me by the hand into Damascus, because the brilliance of the light had blinded me.

[12]"A man named Ananias came to see me. He was a devout observer of the law and highly respected by all the Jews living there. [13]He stood beside me and said, 'Brother Saul, receive your sight!' And at that very moment I was able to see him.

[14]"Then he said: 'The God of our fathers has chosen you to know his will and to see the Righteous One and to hear words from his mouth. [15]You will be his witness to all men of what you have seen and heard. [16]And now what are you waiting for? Get up, be baptized and wash your sins away, calling on his name.'

[17]"When I returned to Jerusalem and was praying at the temple, I fell into a trance [18]and saw the Lord speaking. 'Quick!' he said to me. 'Leave Jerusalem immediately, because they will not accept your testimony about me.'

[19]" 'Lord,' I replied, 'these men know that I went from one synagogue to another to imprison and beat those who believe in you. [20]And when the blood of your martyr[s] Stephen was shed, I stood there giving my approval and guarding the clothes of those who were killing him.'

[21]"Then the Lord said to me, 'Go; I will send you far away to the Gentiles.' "

Paul the Roman Citizen

[22]The crowd listened to Paul until he said this. Then they raised their voices and shouted, "Rid the earth of him! He's not fit to live!"

[23]As they were shouting and throwing off their cloaks and flinging dust into the air, [24]the commander ordered Paul to be taken into the barracks. He directed that he be flogged and questioned in order to find out why the people were shouting at him like this. [25]As they stretched him out to flog him, Paul said to the centurion standing there, "Is it legal for you to flog

[s]20 Or *witness*

a Roman citizen who hasn't even been found guilty?"

²⁶When the centurion heard this, he went to the commander and reported it. "What are you going to do?" he asked. "This man is a Roman citizen."

²⁷The commander went to Paul and asked, "Tell me, are you a Roman citizen?"

"Yes, I am," he answered.

²⁸Then the commander said, "I had to pay a big price for my citizenship."

"But I was born a citizen," Paul replied.

²⁹Those who were about to question him withdrew immediately. The commander himself was alarmed when he realized that he had put Paul, a Roman citizen, in chains.

Before the Sanhedrin

³⁰The next day, since the commander wanted to find out exactly why Paul was being accused by the Jews, he released him and ordered the chief priests and all the Sanhedrin to assemble. Then he brought Paul and had him stand before them.

23 Paul looked straight at the Sanhedrin and said, "My brothers, I have fulfilled my duty to God in all good conscience to this day." ²At this the high priest Ananias ordered those standing near Paul to strike him on the mouth. ³Then Paul said to him, "God will strike you, you whitewashed wall! You sit there to judge me according to the law, yet you yourself violate the law by commanding that I be struck!"

⁴Those who were standing near Paul said, "You dare to insult God's high priest?"

⁵Paul replied, "Brothers, I did not realize that he was the high priest; for it is written: 'Do not speak evil about the ruler of your people.'"

⁶Then Paul, knowing that some of them were Sadducees and the others Pharisees, called out in the Sanhedrin, "My brothers, I am a Pharisee, the son of a Pharisee. I stand on trial because of my hope in the resurrection of the dead." ⁷When he said this, a dispute broke out between the Pharisees and the Sadducees, and the assembly was divided. ⁸(The Sadducees say that there is no resurrection, and that there are neither angels nor spirits, but the Pharisees acknowledge them all.)

⁹There was a great uproar, and some of the teachers of the law who were Pharisees stood up and argued vigorously. "We find nothing wrong with this man," they said. "What if a spirit or an angel has spoken to him?" ¹⁰The dispute became so violent that the commander was afraid Paul would be torn to pieces by them. He ordered the troops to go down and take him away from them by force and bring him into the barracks.

¹¹The following night the Lord stood near Paul and said, "Take courage! As you have testified about me in Jerusalem, so you must also testify in Rome."

REFLECT: 1. What's one of the worst things anyone has ever said to you? How did it affect you then? What scars remain? How has God helped heal those scars? **2.** After having been flogged before, what do you think Paul was thinking when flogging was threatened again? What is one thing that would be extremely difficult for you to endure for the cause of Christ? Why? **3.** What do you appreciate most about being a citizen of your country? About being a citizen in God's kingdom?

OPEN: What's one of the biggest disputes you've ever been involved in? How many people got involved before it was over?

DIG: 1. Why would Paul's statement in 23:1 make the high priest so angry? What does this say about his view of Paul? **2.** What do you learn about Paul's respect for the Law from verse 5? Does his statement here support or discredit the charges against him? How? **3.** How does Paul split the assembly? Why do you think he does this? How does this passage compare with Luke 20:27-40? **4.** What effect does the split have on Paul's case? If you were the commander, what would you conclude after this meeting? **5.** How does Paul's appearance before the Sanhedrin compare with Jesus' appearance before them? Who had the strongest position from a political standpoint? How does the commander compare with Pilate in his relationship to the Sanhedrin? **6.** How would the Lord's message in verse 11 encourage Paul? What do you learn about God in this verse? About his relationship with Paul?

REFLECT: 1. How important for the Christian is respect for God's law? Is this different from Paul's day? Why? **2.** If the Lord came tomorrow night to your house and stood beside you, what message do you think he'd bring? Why? **3.** Where is your Rome—the next important step in your spiritual pilgrimage? How is God preparing you for this?

⁵ Exodus 22:28

OPEN: When you were growing up, who was one of your favorite uncles? Why?

DIG: How determined are those opposed to Paul to bring harm to him? What position does this put Paul in? What relation is there between Paul's position and God's words in verse 11? How would this affect Paul's attitude toward his situation?

REFLECT: 1. How do you think the world would be different today if Paul's nephew had not taken a risk and become involved? What were his risks? What do you learn from his courage and involvement that you can apply to your life? **2.** What are some factors that keep you from getting involved in the lives of others? Of these, which are legitimate? Which are not? How do you determine when to get involved and when not? **3.** Who are some people who have gotten involved in your life? How? **4.** How has God protected you this week? Why do you think God takes such good care of you? How will you thank God for his protection?

OPEN: What's one of the most memorable forced marches in which you've ever participated (a military march, a camping trip, etc.)? Why was this so memorable?

DIG: 1. How extensive an operation does the commander organize to protect Paul? Why do you think he uses such a large force for one man? What do you learn about the concerns of the Roman Empire from this? About its strength? **2.** Where is Caesarea? How far is it from Jerusalem? **3.** Does it surprise you that the governor lives in Caesaria rather than in Jerusalem? What does this tell you about the relative importance of the two cities? What does it tell you about the concerns of the Romans? About the concerns of the authors of the Bible? **4.** How important is Roman justice to the spread of the gospel? Do you think it is just a coincidence that God chose this time in history to build his church? **5.** In chapters 21-23, whom has God used to take care of Paul? What do you conclude from that?

54

The Plot to Kill Paul

¹²The next morning the Jews formed a conspiracy and bound themselves with an oath not to eat or drink until they had killed Paul. ¹³More than forty men were involved in this plot. ¹⁴They went to the chief priests and elders and said, "We have taken a solemn oath not to eat anything until we have killed Paul. ¹⁵Now then, you and the Sanhedrin petition the commander to bring him before you on the pretext of wanting more accurate information about his case. We are ready to kill him before he gets here."

¹⁶But when the son of Paul's sister heard of this plot, he went into the barracks and told Paul.

¹⁷Then Paul called one of the centurions and said, "Take this young man to the commander; he has something to tell him." ¹⁸So he took him to the commander.

The centurion said, "Paul, the prisoner, sent for me and asked me to bring this young man to you because he has something to tell you."

¹⁹The commander took the young man by the hand, drew him aside and asked, "What is it you want to tell me?"

²⁰He said: "The Jews have agreed to ask you to bring Paul before the Sanhedrin tomorrow on the pretext of wanting more accurate information about him. ²¹Don't give in to them, because more than forty of them are waiting in ambush for him. They have taken an oath not to eat or drink until they have killed him. They are ready now, waiting for your consent to their request."

²²The commander dismissed the young man and cautioned him, "Don't tell anyone that you have reported this to me."

Paul Transferred to Caesarea

²³Then he called two of his centurions and ordered them, "Get ready a detachment of two hundred soldiers, seventy horsemen and two hundred spearmen" to go to Caesarea at nine tonight. ²⁴Provide mounts for Paul so that he may be taken safely to Governor Felix."

²⁵He wrote a letter as follows:

²⁶Claudius Lysias,

To His Excellency, Governor Felix:

Greetings.

²⁷This man was seized by the Jews and they were about to kill him, but I came with my troops and rescued him, for I had learned that he is a Roman citizen. ²⁸I wanted to know why they were accusing him, so I brought him to their Sanhedrin. ²⁹I found that the accusation had to do with questions about their law, but there was no charge against him that deserved death or imprisonment. ³⁰When I was informed of a plot to be carried out against the man,

"23 The meaning of the Greek for this word is uncertain.

I sent him to you at once. I also ordered his accusers to present to you their case against him.

³¹So the soldiers, carrying out their orders, took Paul with them during the night and brought him as far as Antipatris. ³²The next day they let the cavalry go on with him, while they returned to the barracks. ³³When the cavalry arrived in Caesarea, they delivered the letter to the governor and handed Paul over to him. ³⁴The governor read the letter and asked what province he was from. Learning that he was from Cilicia, ³⁵he said, "I will hear your case when your accusers get here." Then he ordered that Paul be kept under guard in Herod's palace.

The Trial Before Felix

24 Five days later the high priest Ananias went down to Caesarea with some of the elders and a lawyer named Tertullus, and they brought their charges against Paul before the governor. ²When Paul was called in, Tertullus presented his case before Felix: "We have enjoyed a long period of peace under you, and your foresight has brought about reforms in this nation. ³Everywhere and in every way, most excellent Felix, we acknowledge this with profound gratitude. ⁴But in order not to weary you further, I would request that you be kind enough to hear us briefly.

⁵"We have found this man to be a troublemaker, stirring up riots among the Jews all over the world. He is a ringleader of the Nazarene sect ⁶and even tried to desecrate the temple; so we seized him. ⁸By⁰ examining him yourself you will be able to learn the truth about all these charges we are bringing against him."

⁹The Jews joined in the accusation, asserting that these things were true.

¹⁰When the governor motioned for him to speak, Paul replied: "I know that for a number of years you have been a judge over this nation; so I gladly make my defense. ¹¹You can easily verify that no more than twelve days ago I went up to Jerusalem to worship. ¹²My accusers did not find me arguing with anyone at the temple, or stirring up a crowd in the synagogues or anywhere else in the city. ¹³And they cannot prove to you the charges they are now making against me. ¹⁴However, I admit that I worship the God of our fathers as a follower of the Way, which they call a sect. I believe everything that agrees with the Law and that is written in the Prophets, ¹⁵and I have the same hope in God as these men, that there will be a resurrection of both the righteous and the wicked. ¹⁶So I strive always to keep my conscience clear before God and man.

¹⁷"After an absence of several years, I came to Jerusalem to bring my people gifts for the poor and to present offerings. ¹⁸I was ceremonially clean when they found me in the temple courts doing this. There was no crowd with me, nor was I involved in any disturbance. ¹⁹But there are some Jews from the province

ᵛ6-8 Some manuscripts him and wanted to judge him according to our law. ⁷But the commander, Lysias, came and with the use of much force snatched him from our hands ⁸and ordered his accusers to come before you. By

REFLECT: Do you think there is a reason that God has placed you at this point in history? In this country? If so, what do you think it is? Have you always taken full advantage of your situation? Why or why not? What could you do this week to make better use of your situation?

OPEN: Who was the greatest peacemaker in your family? How did he or she work at achieving peace?

DIG: 1. Of the four charges brought against Paul in this trial, which are true? How might they all seem true to Ananias and Tertullus? How would this make the trial more difficult to judge? **2.** Which of the charges against Paul would Felix be most concerned about? Why? How would the letter he received from Jerusalem (23: 26-30) be likely to affect his judgment on this matter? Why? **3.** What does Paul mean in verses 15-16? How does this relate to the charges against him? What does it say about Paul as a man? **4.** In verses 17-21, how does Paul answer the major concern of Felix? How would the truth of the statements in these verses damage the case against Paul? What outcome do you think Paul was expecting at this point? **5.** How does Felix's greed affect the decision? How do you think Paul was feeling during the two years he was in prison without any real progress in his case?

REFLECT: 1. What is inconvenient for you about being a Christian? **2.** What's the difference between being "well acquainted with the Way" and being a believer? How long were you well acquainted before you became a believer? **3.** In what ways have you been like Felix? If you could pass on a word of wisdom to Felix, what would you say? **4.** What have you learned from Paul about grace under pressure? **5.** What are your prisons? How have you been able to serve Christ while in prison? What do you learn about prison from Paul and from God's experience in your life?

of Asia, who ought to be here before you and bring charges if they have anything against me. 20Or these who are here should state what crime they found in me when I stood before the Sanhedrin— 21unless it was this one thing I shouted as I stood in their presence: 'It is concerning the resurrection of the dead that I am on trial before you today.' "

22Then Felix, who was well acquainted with the Way, adjourned the proceedings. "When Lysias the commander comes," he said, "I will decide your case." 23He ordered the centurion to keep Paul under guard but to give him some freedom and permit his friends to take care of his needs.

24Several days later Felix came with his wife Drusilla, who was a Jewess. He sent for Paul and listened to him as he spoke about faith in Christ Jesus. 25As Paul discoursed on righteousness, self-control and the judgment to come, Felix was afraid and said, "That's enough for now! You may leave. When I find it convenient, I will send for you." 26At the same time he was hoping that Paul would offer him a bribe, so he sent for him frequently and talked with him.

27When two years had passed, Felix was succeeded by Porcius Festus, but because Felix wanted to grant a favor to the Jews, he left Paul in prison.

The Trial Before Festus

25 Three days after arriving in the province, Festus went up from Caesarea to Jerusalem, 2where the chief priests and Jewish leaders appeared before him and presented the charges against Paul. 3They urgently requested Festus, as a favor to them, to have Paul transferred to Jerusalem, for they were preparing an ambush to kill him along the way. 4Festus answered, "Paul is being held at Caesarea, and I myself am going there soon. 5Let some of your leaders come with me and press charges against the man there, if he has done anything wrong."

6After spending eight or ten days with them, he went down to Caesarea, and the next day he convened the court and ordered that Paul be brought before him. 7When Paul appeared, the Jews who had come down from Jerusalem stood around him, bringing many serious charges against him, which they could not prove.

8Then Paul made his defense: "I have done nothing wrong against the law of the Jews or against the temple or against Caesar."

9Festus, wishing to do the Jews a favor, said to Paul, "Are you willing to go up to Jerusalem and stand trial before me there on these charges?"

10Paul answered: "I am now standing before Caesar's court, where I ought to be tried. I have not done any wrong to the Jews, as you yourself know very well. 11If, however, I am guilty of doing anything deserving death, I do not refuse to die. But if the charges brought against me by these Jews are not true, no one has the right to hand me over to them. I appeal to Caesar!"

12After Festus had conferred with his council, he declared: "You have appealed to Caesar. To Caesar you will go!"

OPEN: Who was one of the toughest school principals you ever had? Why?

DIG: 1. Why do you think the chief priests act so quickly against Paul? Why do you think they continue to make charges that they cannot prove? What does this have to do with verse 3? What does this say about the strength of their desires concerning Paul? **2.** What has been Paul's defense all along? If his statements in Acts 24:13 and 25:10 are true, why is he still imprisoned? What do you learn from this? **3.** How does Paul's appeal to Caesar thwart the plans of the Jerusalem leaders? Why do you think Paul waits so long (two years) to make this appeal? How does verse 9 support your answer?

REFLECT: 1. What are some circumstances that have ambushed you in your spiritual pilgrimage? What happened? What have you learned? **2.** If someone wanted to prove that you were a Christian, would there be enough evidence to convict you? Why or why not? **3.** When you think about your own death, what fears do you have?

Festus Consults King Agrippa

[13]A few days later King Agrippa and Bernice arrived at Caesarea to pay their respects to Festus. [14]Since they were spending many days there, Festus discussed Paul's case with the king. He said: "There is a man here whom Felix left as a prisoner. [15]When I went to Jerusalem, the chief priests and elders of the Jews brought charges against him and asked that he be condemned.

[16]"I told them that it is not the Roman custom to hand over any man before he has faced his accusers and has had an opportunity to defend himself against their charges. [17]When they came here with me, I did not delay the case, but convened the court the next day and ordered the man to be brought in. [18]When his accusers got up to speak, they did not charge him with any of the crimes I had expected. [19]Instead, they had some points of dispute with him about their own religion and about a dead man named Jesus who Paul claimed was alive. [20]I was at a loss how to investigate such matters; so I asked if he would be willing to go to Jerusalem and stand trial there on these charges. [21]When Paul made his appeal to be held over for the Emperor's decision, I ordered him held until I could send him to Caesar."

[22]Then Agrippa said to Festus, "I would like to hear this man myself."

He replied, "Tomorrow you will hear him."

Paul Before Agrippa

[23]The next day Agrippa and Bernice came with great pomp and entered the audience room with the high ranking officers and the leading men of the city. At the command of Festus, Paul was brought in. [24]Festus said: "King Agrippa, and all who are present with us, you see this man! The whole Jewish community has petitioned me about him in Jerusalem and here in Caesarea, shouting that he ought not to live any longer. [25]I found he had done nothing deserving of death, but because he made his appeal to the Emperor I decided to send him to Rome. [26]But I have nothing definite to write to His Majesty about him. Therefore I have brought him before all of you, and especially before you, King Agrippa, so that as a result of this investigation I may have something to write. [27]For I think it is unreasonable to send on a prisoner without specifying the charges against him."

26 Then Agrippa said to Paul, "You have permission to speak for yourself."

So Paul motioned with his hand and began his defense: [2]"King Agrippa, I consider myself fortunate to stand before you today as I make my defense against all the accusations of the Jews, [3]and especially so because you are well acquainted with all the Jewish customs and controversies. Therefore, I beg you to listen to me patiently.

[4]"The Jews all know the way I have lived ever since I was a child, from the beginning of my life in my own country, and also in Jerusalem. [5]They have known me for a long time and can testify, if they are willing, that according to the strictest sect of our religion, I lived as a Pharisee. [6]And now it is because of my hope in what God has promised our fathers that I am on trial today. [7]This is the promise our twelve tribes are hoping to see

self? In explaining the gospel? **6.** How has God used Paul's circumstances to proclaim the gospel to people in power (chapters 23-26)?

REFLECT: 1. Paul considered himself a servant and a witness. In what way is God's call to you similar to his call to Paul? Different? **2.** If you were telling your story, into how many different phases would you divide it? What are these parts? What was one highlight during each phase? **3.** What confidence does the fact that the gospel is "true and reasonable" and "not done in a corner" give you? **4.** If you were in Paul's position, could you share the gospel? Why or why not? **5.** Under what circumstances do you feel most comfortable sharing the gospel? Why? What do you learn about sharing the gospel in this passage? How can you put this into practice today?

fulfilled as they earnestly serve God day and night. O king, it is because of this hope that the Jews are accusing me. [8]Why should any of you consider it incredible that God raises the dead?

[9]"I too was convinced that I ought to do all that was possible to oppose the name of Jesus of Nazareth. [10]And that is just what I did in Jerusalem. On the authority of the chief priests I put many of the saints in prison, and when they were put to death, I cast my vote against them. [11]Many a time I went from one synagogue to another to have them punished, and I tried to force them to blaspheme. In my obsession against them, I even went to foreign cities to persecute them.

[12]"On one of these journeys I was going to Damascus with the authority and commission of the chief priests. [13]About noon, O king, as I was on the road, I saw a light from heaven, brighter than the sun, blazing around me and my companions. [14]We all fell to the ground, and I heard a voice saying to me in Aramaic,[w] 'Saul, Saul, why do you persecute me? It is hard for you to kick against the goads.'

[15]"Then I asked, 'Who are you, Lord?'

" 'I am Jesus, whom you are persecuting,' the Lord replied. [16]'Now get up and stand on your feet. I have appeared to you to appoint you as a servant and as a witness of what you have seen of me and what I will show you. [17]I will rescue you from your own people and from the Gentiles. I am sending you to them [18]to open their eyes and turn them from darkness to light, and from the power of Satan to God, so that they may receive forgiveness of sins and a place among those who are sanctified by faith in me.'

[19]"So then, King Agrippa, I was not disobedient to the vision from heaven. [20]First to those in Damascus, then to those in Jerusalem and in all Judea, and to the Gentiles also, I preached that they should repent and turn to God and prove their repentance by their deeds. [21]That is why the Jews seized me in the temple courts and tried to kill me. [22]But I have had God's help to this very day, and so I stand here and testify to small and great alike. I am saying nothing beyond what the prophets and Moses said would happen— [23]that the Christ[x] would suffer and, as the first to rise from the dead, would proclaim light to his own people and to the Gentiles."

[24]At this point Festus interrupted Paul's defense. "You are out of your mind, Paul!" he shouted. "Your great learning is driving you insane."

[25]"I am not insane, most excellent Festus," Paul replied. "What I am saying is true and reasonable. [26]The king is familiar with these things, and I can speak freely to him. I am convinced that none of this has escaped his notice, because it was not done in a corner. [27]King Agrippa, do you believe the prophets? I know you do."

[28]Then Agrippa said to Paul, "Do you think that in such a short time you can persuade me to be a Christian?"

[29]Paul replied, "Short time or long—I pray God that not only

w14 Or *Hebrew*   *x23* Or *Messiah*

you but all who are listening to me today may become what I am, except for these chains.''

[30]The king rose, and with him the governor and Bernice and those sitting with them. [31]They left the room, and while talking with one another, they said, "This man is not doing anything that deserves death or imprisonment.''

[32]Agrippa said to Festus, "This man could have been set free if he had not appealed to Caesar.''

Paul Sails for Rome

27 When it was decided that we would sail for Italy, Paul and some other prisoners were handed over to a centurion named Julius, who belonged to the Imperial Regiment. [2]We boarded a ship from Adramyttium about to sail for ports along the coast of the province of Asia, and we put out to sea. Aristarchus, a Macedonian from Thessalonica, was with us.

[3]The next day we landed at Sidon; and Julius, in kindness to Paul, allowed him to go to his friends so they might provide for his needs. [4]From there we put out to sea again and passed to the lee of Cyprus because the winds were against us. [5]When we had sailed across the open sea off the coast of Cilicia and Pamphylia, we landed at Myra in Lycia. [6]There the centurion found an Alexandrian ship sailing for Italy and put us on board. [7]We made slow headway for many days and had difficulty arriving off Cnidus. When the wind did not allow us to hold our course, we sailed to the lee of Crete, opposite Salmone. [8]We moved along the coast with difficulty and came to a place called Fair Havens, near the town of Lasea.

[9]Much time had been lost, and sailing had already become dangerous because by now it was after the Fast.[y] So Paul warned them, [10]"Men, I can see that our voyage is going to be disastrous and bring great loss to ship and cargo, and to our own lives also.'' [11]But the centurion, instead of listening to what Paul said, followed the advice of the pilot and of the owner of the ship. [12]Since the harbor was unsuitable to winter in, the majority decided that we should sail on, hoping to reach Phoenix and winter there. This was a harbor in Crete, facing both southwest and northwest.

The Storm

[13]When a gentle south wind began to blow, they thought they had obtained what they wanted; so they weighed anchor and sailed along the shore of Crete. [14]Before very long, a wind of hurricane force, called the "northeaster," swept down from the island. [15]The ship was caught by the storm and could not head into the wind; so we gave way to it and were driven along. [16]As we passed to the lee of a small island called Cauda, we were hardly able to make the lifeboat secure. [17]When the men had hoisted it aboard, they passed ropes under the ship itself to hold it together. Fearing that they would run aground on the sandbars of Syrtis, they lowered the sea anchor and let the ship be driven along. [18]We took such a violent battering from the storm

OPEN: What was the worst vacation you ever took with your family? What made it so bad?

DIG: 1. Trace Paul's trip on a map. What do you know about these places? **2.** Who is traveling with Paul at this point? Who's in charge? What does Luke say about the man? **3.** What difficulties are encountered? How does Luke describe the situation? Of what does Paul warn? Who disagrees with Paul? Probably on what basis? What is the final decision?

REFLECT: 1. From where did unexpected kindness come to Paul in this story? How has unexpected kindness come to you in the past month? **2.** Who are some new and different people in your life who have made a difference this year? How? Whose advice do you wish you had followed at one time in your life? What happened because you didn't? How did God continue to work with you despite your unwise decision?

OPEN: When were you the most seasick, carsick, or airsick in your life? What is your most vivid impression of this time?

DIG: 1. How would you describe the progressive deterioration of the ship, the cargo, the passengers, and the crew? How bad does the situation get? **2.** In the midst of their hopelessness, what word does Paul bring? Who was God's message primarily designed to comfort—Paul or the crew? Why? How much faith do you think the crew had in Paul at this point? Why?

y9 That is, the Day of Atonement (Yom Kippur)

that the next day they began to throw the cargo overboard. [19]On the third day, they threw the ship's tackle overboard with their own hands. [20]When neither sun nor stars appeared for many days and the storm continued raging, we finally gave up all hope of being saved.

[21]After the men had gone a long time without food, Paul stood up before them and said: "Men, you should have taken my advice not to sail from Crete; then you would have spared yourselves this damage and loss. [22]But now I urge you to keep up your courage, because not one of you will be lost; only the ship will be destroyed. [23]Last night an angel of the God whose I am and whom I serve stood beside me [24]and said, 'Do not be afraid, Paul. You must stand trial before Caesar; and God has graciously given you the lives of all who sail with you.' [25]So keep up your courage, men, for I have faith in God that it will happen just as he told me. [26]Nevertheless, we must run aground on some island."

The Shipwreck

[27]On the fourteenth night we were still being driven across the Adriatic[z] Sea, when about midnight the sailors sensed they were approaching land. [28]They took soundings and found that the water was a hundred and twenty feet[a] deep. A short time later they took soundings again and found it was ninety feet[b] deep. [29]Fearing that we would be dashed against the rocks, they dropped four anchors from the stern and prayed for daylight. [30]In an attempt to escape from the ship, the sailors let the lifeboat down into the sea, pretending they were going to lower some anchors from the bow. [31]Then Paul said to the centurion and the soldiers, "Unless these men stay with the ship, you cannot be saved." [32]So the soldiers cut the ropes that held the lifeboat and let it fall away.

[33]Just before dawn Paul urged them all to eat. "For the last fourteen days," he said, "you have been in constant suspense and have gone without food—you haven't eaten anything. [34]Now I urge you to take some food. You need it to survive. Not one of you will lose a single hair from his head." [35]After he said this, he took some bread and gave thanks to God in front of them all. Then he broke it and began to eat. [36]They were all encouraged and ate some food themselves. [37]Altogether there were 276 of us on board. [38]When they had eaten as much as they wanted, they lightened the ship by throwing the grain into the sea.

[39]When daylight came, they did not recognize the land, but they saw a bay with a sandy beach, where they decided to run the ship aground if they could. [40]Cutting loose the anchors, they left them in the sea and at the same time untied the ropes that held the rudders. Then they hoisted the foresail to the wind and made for the beach. [41]But the ship struck a sandbar and ran aground. The bow stuck fast and would not move, and the stern was broken to pieces by the pounding of the surf.

z27 In ancient times-the name referred to an area extending well south of Italy.
a28 Greek *twenty orguias* (about 37 meters)   b28 Greek *fifteen orguias* (about 27 meters)

⁴²The soldiers planned to kill the prisoners to prevent any of them from swimming away and escaping. ⁴³But the centurion wanted to spare Paul's life and kept them from carrying out their plan. He ordered those who could swim to jump overboard first and get to land. ⁴⁴The rest were to get there on planks or on pieces of the ship. In this way everyone reached land in safety.

Ashore on Malta

28 Once safely on shore, we found out that the island was called Malta. ²The islanders showed us unusual kindness. They built a fire and welcomed us all because it was raining and cold. ³Paul gathered a pile of brushwood and, as he put it on the fire, a viper, driven out by the heat, fastened itself on his hand. ⁴When the islanders saw the snake hanging from his hand, they said to each other, "This man must be a murderer; for though he escaped from the sea, Justice has not allowed him to live." ⁵But Paul shook the snake off into the fire and suffered no ill effects. ⁶The people expected him to swell up or suddenly fall dead, but after waiting a long time and seeing nothing unusual happen to him, they changed their minds and said he was a god.

⁷There was an estate nearby that belonged to Publius, the chief official of the island. He welcomed us to his home and for three days entertained us hospitably. ⁸His father was sick in bed, suffering from fever and dysentery. Paul went in to see him and, after prayer, placed his hands on him and healed him. ⁹When this had happened, the rest of the sick on the island came and were cured. ¹⁰They honored us in many ways and when we were ready to sail, they furnished us with the supplies we needed.

Arrival at Rome

¹¹After three months we put out to sea in a ship that had wintered in the island. It was an Alexandrian ship with the figurehead of the twin gods Castor and Pollux. ¹²We put in at Syracuse and stayed there three days. ¹³From there we set sail and arrived at Rhegium. The next day the south wind came up, and on the following day we reached Puteoli. ¹⁴There we found some brothers who invited us to spend a week with them. And so we came to Rome. ¹⁵The brothers there had heard that we were coming, and they traveled as far as the Forum of Appius and the Three Taverns to meet us. At the sight of these men Paul thanked God and was encouraged. ¹⁶When we got to Rome, Paul was allowed to live by himself, with a soldier to guard him.

Paul Preaches at Rome Under Guard

¹⁷Three days later he called together the leaders of the Jews. When they had assembled, Paul said to them: "My brothers, although I have done nothing against our people or against the customs of our ancestors, I was arrested in Jerusalem and handed over to the Romans. ¹⁸They examined me and wanted to release me, because I was not guilty of any crime deserving death. ¹⁹But when the Jews objected, I was compelled to appeal to Caesar—not that I had any charge to bring against my own people. ²⁰For this reason I have asked to see you and talk with

OPEN: What is one memory of a snake you have? What happened?

DIG: 1. Why do you think God has allowed the things in Acts 27:1-28:9 happen? **2.** If you were one of the soldiers on this journey to Rome, would you consider it a successful trip? Why or why not? If you were Paul, would you consider this trip a success? Why or why not? **3.** After all this time with Paul, how do you think the centurion feels about Paul and the Christian faith? Why?

REFLECT: 1. How has God used a disaster in your life for ministry? What have you learned from this? **2.** Whom is God prompting you to see or write? What could you do this week to reach out to that person? **3.** How difficult is it for you to accept hospitality and to receive help? What makes you that way? How do you think God would like to change you?

DIG: 1. How do you think these travelers feel after finally arriving in Rome? **2.** Do you think Paul needed the encouragement he received in verse 15? Why or why not?

REFLECT: 1. In what area of your life has God given you special encouragement this week? How important is this kind of encouragement for you? What does it do for your faith? **2.** How important is it to encourage our spiritual leaders? What can you do this week to encourage your spiritual leaders?

OPEN: Of the homes you've lived in, which two are your favorites? Why? In whose home, other than your own, do you feel most comfortable? Why?

DIG: 1. Why do you think Paul calls this meeting with the Jews of Rome? Is it surprising that they have not heard of Paul? Why or why not? **2.** How would you characterize the attitude of the Roman Jews toward Paul? How does this compare to the attitude of the leaders from Jerusalem? Why do you think there is such a difference? **3.** In what ways are the words of Isaiah in verses 26-27 an accurate description of the Jewish response to Christianity? Why would this passage from Isaiah and the words of verse 28 cause the Jews of Rome to leave? **4.** In what ways is verse 28 an accurate description of the controversy and conflicts found in the Book of Acts? How is it an accurate summary? **5.** What do you see as the most outstanding example of God at work in the Book of Acts? Write your own summary paragraph for Acts.

REFLECT: 1. How would you characterize the ministry you have in your home? What do you like best about using your home to reach out to others? How do you think you could use it more effectively? **2.** What are some things that bother your non-Christian friends about the faith? How do you help them to overcome those barriers? **3.** If your life were a chapter in the Book of Acts, what do you think it would be about? What would you like it to say? In what way is your life a continuation of the Book of Acts? How does this make you feel? What does it make you want to do? Why?

you. It is because of the hope of Israel that I am bound with this chain."

²¹They replied, "We have not received any letters from Judea concerning you, and none of the brothers who have come from there has reported or said anything bad about you. ²²But we want to hear what your views are, for we know that people everywhere are talking against this sect."

²³They arranged to meet Paul on a certain day, and came in even larger numbers to the place where he was staying. From morning till evening he explained and declared to them the kingdom of God and tried to convince them about Jesus from the Law of Moses and from the Prophets. ²⁴Some were convinced by what he said, but others would not believe. ²⁵They disagreed among themselves and began to leave after Paul had made this final statement: "The Holy Spirit spoke the truth to your forefathers when he said through Isaiah the prophet:

²⁶" 'Go to this people and say,
   "You will be ever hearing but never understanding;
      you will be ever seeing but never perceiving."
²⁷For this people's heart has become calloused;
   they hardly hear with their ears,
   and they have closed their eyes.
Otherwise they might see with their eyes,
   hear with their ears,
   understand with their hearts
   and turn, and I would heal them.' ᶜ

²⁸"Therefore I want you to know that God's salvation has been sent to the Gentiles, and they will listen!" ᵈ

³⁰For two whole years Paul stayed there in his own rented house and welcomed all who came to see him. ³¹Boldly and without hindrance he preached the kingdom of God and taught about the Lord Jesus Christ.

ᶜ27 Isaiah 6:9,10   ᵈ28 Some manuscripts *listen!"* ²⁹*After he said this, the Jews left, arguing vigorously among themselves.*

NOTES

NOTES